❖

FAITH ADVENTURES

❖

By

Vicki Garza

xulon
PRESS

"We were spellbound reading this profound story of the Lord's faithfulness when we choose to obey the unction of the Holy Spirit. This story is insightful, motivating and challenging. This book will put a desire in you to reach your destiny in the Lord. IT WILL CHANGE YOUR LIFE!!!..."

Bob and Anne Snelling, Founders
Snelling and Snelling
Plano, TX

"Vicki Garza's book is a thrilling account of God's faithfulness and one woman's daring adventure of faith. Your heart will be lifted to believe for God's supernatural actions for you and your family. You will be challenged to obey every urging of His Spirit in your life."

David Shibley, President
Global Advance
Dallas, TX

"Some people feel the Lord's hand gently. Others ignore his presence altogether. Then, there are those to whom the Lord speaks directly and forcefully and they, in turn, have the faith to respond. In a gripping, adventure-filled journey, this book takes you through a story of faith that is surprising, uplifting and truly inspiring."

Dr. Lynn Thurston
Naples, NY

"Thank you for sharing your wonderful book of the testimony of your life. God is definitely alive and working. What a great story. Blessings with your book. God will use your story to touch lives."

Shelly Millheim
Fort Worth, TX

Dedication

To Paco, the Love of my Life

I dedicate this book to my amazing husband, Paco, who the Lord in His wisdom handpicked from the foundation of the world to be my lifelong love.

His tireless dedication to me in the face of some very precarious situations has given me the strength and freedom to be who God created me to be.

I will love you forever, honey.

Contents

❦

Acknowledgements

I am deeply grateful for the help and encouragement of several key individuals in getting this book to the public. When the Lord first called me to write what He had done in my life, I was thinking it would be a wonderful legacy to hand down to my children, their children and future generations of our family. Once I finished and passed it on to a few friends, I was convicted the Lord wanted my story to be shared with the world.

I want to first of all thank my mom, who was the first to read the book, and whose excitement was contagious. I was reminded of the many times she encouraged me as a child to never let others opinions of me inhibit me from being myself. Her advice that excuses are not necessary - your friends do not need them and your enemies will not believe you anyway - has taken me far in life.

The second person to read the book was my dear friend from Naples, Edda Pulver, who convinced me my story had to be shared with all who would listen. Her friendship and enthusiasm has truly been an inspiration.

When I was still not sure of whether or not to publish this book, I was struck by the testimony of Heather French Hunter, who had the courage to share the pain and the consequences of her disobedience to the Holy Spirit on *Oprah* this past November, to an audience of millions.

As my heart broke for her, I found a renewed sense of determination to share the other side of the story – the unspeakable joy of living in obedience to the unction of the Holy Spirit. I pray Heather will know that her obedience in sharing her message with America on prime time TV was a major coup in the heavenlies for the Lord. Thank you, Heather.

I want to thank Joe Slaughter for leading me to Eva Shaw, who gave me great advice and encouraged me to hang in there when I was feeling overwhelmed with the process of finding a publisher.

And my deep thanks to Allison Skidgel, a stranger I met on an airplane, for sending me the e-mail, urging me to finish the manuscript I had shelved. Her message prompting me to complete the book - "people need to know" - haunted me until I had finished. I knew our meeting on a flight from Dallas to Chicago was a divine appointment from God.

I would be remiss if I did not thank Dr. Larry Lea, our mentor in the Lord, whose seeds are still bringing forth fruit in our lives twenty years later.

Finally, I want to thank Ray Baron, my editor, friend and greatest encourager of all. I shudder to think where we would be today if he had not been faithful to share the Lord with us. This story begins with him and ends with him, so the circle is complete.

About the Amplified Bible*

❧

"The Amplified Bible, first released in its entirety in 1964, attempts to go beyond the traditional 'word-for-word' concept of translation to bring out the richness of the Hebrew and Greek languages. Its purpose is to reveal, together with the single English word equivalent to each key Hebrew and Greek word, any other clarifying meanings that may be concealed by the traditional translation method.

Perhaps for the first time in an English version of the Bible, the full meaning of the key words in the original text is available for the reader. In a sense, the creative use of amplification merely helps the reader comprehend what the Hebrew and Greek listener instinctively understood (as a matter of course)."

FOREWORD

God Is Waiting For Us

❧

I have been intending to write this book for a long time. Over the past twenty years, I have seen God move in my life in a way that few Christians ever experience. Every time I have seriously contemplated getting started on the manuscript, one thing has stopped me: a concern that somehow my story would be misconstrued as a way to bring fame, fortune or glory to myself.

Given the fact that I have a background in marketing, public relations and promotions, that fear is not unfounded. I am promotional by nature. Therefore, I feel I must begin this book with a statement that explains that this book is not about what I have done and me. I feel compelled to tell my story with a level of honesty that will, over the pages, reveal my complete unworthiness to experience God's anointing and favor in my life.

Before becoming a Christian, my life was average. I was an underachieving individual whose life was supercharged with faith when I gave my life to Christ. In the Bible, I have found great strength in the promises of God. Taking God's Word at face value has empowered me to live a spirit-led and God-inspired life.

I pray this book will bring encouragement to all of the underdogs out there who dream of doing great things for God, regardless of their place in life or lack of education. God is waiting for us to believe Him for great things – abundantly above all we could dream or ask. His desire is that our lives are living testimonies of His love and faithfulness.

May my story encourage, inspire and motivate all believers to be all that they can be in God. The Lord will bless you as you walk in His wisdom and revelation power (Ephesians 1:15-17).

— Vicki Garza, December, 2003

CHAPTER 1

Delivered Out Of The Miry Clay

❧

"You'll never believe what this guy from work told me today," Paco exclaimed excitedly as he walked through the door. Paco, not ordinarily a highly excitable person, was noticeably animated. His big brown eyes were unusually bright.

I was curious. I could not imagine what anyone could tell Paco to get him so riled up. He shifted his tall, slender body from one foot to the other, as though he was trying to get comfortable.

"Remember I told you about my friend, Ray Baron, who keeps a Bible on his desk and talks to me about Jesus whenever I go into his office? Today, he told me Jesus is coming back again."

I stopped what I was doing in the kitchen and moved into the tiny living room to be closer to Paco. A chill had come over me and I needed to feel his warmth. Nearly a foot shorter than him, I suddenly felt very small.

"What does he mean, Jesus is coming back again?" I asked softly.

The chill had turned to full fledge goose bumps. I realized I was actually holding my breath. Tears began to well up in my light green eyes.

I was not even sure I believed in Jesus at all. When I was younger, I wanted to believe in Jesus. I had always believed in God, but the verdict was still out in my mind as to whether or not Jesus ever even lived.

Now at 22, I was not as impressionable as I was growing up in a sheltered, rural community in Upstate New York. I was a sophisticated city girl now. I was not about to be rushed into believing anything.

My thoughts moved back to Paco and his excitement. We had been dating for four years and were getting married in six months. Coming from very different backgrounds, he as a Catholic and I as a Methodist, we had talked at length about the God of the universe we both believed created the world.

However, we had told each other neither of us was religious. We both had experienced varying degrees of hypocrisy within our churches growing up and had consciously chosen to remain neutral in the area of religion.

Somehow, though, I could tell by his voice, this meant a lot to him. His friend had obviously had an effect on him, so I decided to remain open-minded for his sake.

"What else did Ray say? Did he mention *when* Jesus is planning to return?"

Paco looked at me with conviction. Running his fingers through his short, dark hair, he seemed anxious as well. "It's all in the Bible, Vicki. He invited us over to his house Friday night to hear all about it. He seems really convinced Jesus is coming back soon for His people. The way he described it to me, Jesus is only coming back for people who really believe in Him and who are living their lives for Him."

"So," I asked, "are you saying if Jesus came back tonight, He wouldn't take us with Him?"

"I don't know. But I've got the gut feeling we wouldn't qualify. What do you think?"

Again my mind was racing. This was terrible news. I did not understand any of it. On the other hand, I sure did not want to be passed up if Jesus was real and this concept of Him coming back to earth to gather up all of His believers was true.

"I think we should go and get all of the details. I definitely want to hear what this guy has to say."

Paco agreed.

It was January 1978. We did go to Ray's house and were disturbed by what he had to say. He was obviously convinced Jesus was coming back soon and felt it was his personal mission to urge all unbelievers he knew to get their lives "right with God" so they could be included in the rapture of the church as it is described in I Thessalonians 4:16,17.

His words haunted me day and night as I racked my brain to find a way to become a believer without giving up the worldly life I loved. All of my life, I had dreamt of living an exciting, city life. If our friend was right, it looked like my shot at living a full, worldly life was short-lived if I wanted to be counted as a believer when Christ returned.

I finally decided I needed more information if I was to make an informed decision. After the meeting, our friend had given us the book The Late, Great Planet Earth by Hal Lindsey. Although I found the book fascinating reading, I was convicted, but not convinced.

Our June wedding came and went. Paco and I discussed Hal Lindsey's ideas casually over coffee, and life went on as usual. The urgency had subsided.

In October, we bought a home and by November, I was pregnant with our first child. Unable to fathom parenthood, we wept together as we groped with our feelings of inadequacy. We both felt we were way too young to be parents. I personally felt inept and totally unprepared.

"I can't even imagine someone calling me 'Mother,' let alone being someone's mother. I just don't know how we'll ever make ends meet. How are we going to do this, Paco?"

Paco just hung his head and stared at the floor. He did not have to say anything. I knew he was just as overwhelmed as I was with the idea. Before we went to bed that night, I looked in his gentle, warm eyes and confessed: "You know what's really bugging me? I have always believed that when I had children, I would tell them the truth about everything I knew to be true. What will we tell this child when it asks us if there's a God or if Jesus is real? It's really important to me that we have real answers for our children. I refuse to just make something up."

Paco was in agreement once again. It was he who made the suggestion: "Let's start going to church and see if they have any answers."

"Church? What church?" My stomach fell to my knees just thinking about it. I really could not even imagine myself in a church looking for answers. I was more of a Bohemian than that. The whole idea sounded so traditional. I bit my lip to fight back the tears. Secretly, I felt church was only for hypocrites. The idea was too radical for me.

Again, Paco persisted. He ran his fingers through my long, auburn hair and pulled me to him. "It's not that bad, Vic. If we don't like the first one we try, we'll just try another. Come on, sweetie. We're going to be a family now. Families go to church."

"Well, okay, I guess we can try one. If we don't like it, I'm not staying. Do you promise to leave if I feel confined?"

"Sure, honey. We can do that."

I turned my back to Paco so he couldn't see my tears. My heart was breaking. My whole life was coming to an abrupt halt. "I'm going to have a baby and we're going to start going to church." It was more than I could fathom. I fell asleep with a foreboding knowledge that life as I had known it was over.

I honestly cannot remember how we found the small Baptist church in Mesquite. Somehow, we must have found out the service times, because I distinctly remember our first visit. I had managed to put the task off for months. Now that I was nearly six months pregnant, I knew the time had come. There were small groups of people milling around in the lobby, greeting each other, chatting excitedly.

"This isn't so bad," I thought. "It feels pretty friendly."

A nice looking couple caught our eye and came over to us. "Howdy. Welcome to our church. Is this your first time here?" the woman drawled in a thick Texan accent.

My eyes moved down to her bulging belly. I wondered how long before her baby was due and if this was her first child, but I did not know how to ask. Paco extended his hand to her and warmly introduced us.

"He's so smooth in a group of strangers," I thought. I wondered if he was as nervous as I was. I was actually feeling light headed and warm. If he was, he did not show it. Within minutes, we were both at ease with this young couple. They invited us to sit with them. We declined the offer. At the end of the service, however, they were quick to spot us and made their move toward us. Sherry had a piece of paper with her name and number on it. She pressed it into my hand. "Call me sometime, okay? I'd love to get together with you. Or maybe the four of us can get together sometime."

It almost felt like she was a salesperson on commission. What was her hurry? I had noticed that a number of the other members of the church had greeted Terry and Sherry as they milled around, so it did not seem like they were hard up for friends. I was feeling rather defensive at the thought of someone trying to befriend me so fast. I muttered some lame excuse and we left immediately. Once outside, I felt much safer. I touched my flushed face. Why was it so hot? What was it that had upset me so much in there? I could not put my finger on it. One thing was for sure: I had never felt more uncomfortable in my life. Next week, I wanted to try a different church.

The weeks came and went and we remained faithful to the small Baptist church, despite my initial reservations. Sherry introduced me to her friends. She would call once in a while to see how I was doing. She was having her first baby, too, but with her parents and siblings in town, she seemed to be far more prepared for the transition. We learned from mutual friends at the church one Sunday that Sherry had a boy. They would be back to church in a few weeks.

Church did not seem the same without Sherry and Terry there. I had begun to look forward to seeing them. The whole ritual was becoming a social habit that I could definitely get used to. I do not even remember any of those first sermons the pastor preached. I was so self-conscious; my mind was on myself most of the time.

Before long, it was my turn to give birth. Little did I know how truly life changing the event was to become for me.

From the day Elisa came into the world on August 4, 1979, my quiet life was hurled into a whirl of activity. Paco immediately returned to work after her birth, and I was confined to our small house in Pleasant Grove. Our tiny abode was to become my own personal prison. Elisa was a good baby most of the time. However, my life was consumed with her minute-by-minute demands. I was breast-feeding, but she was getting skinnier by the day. I slept when she slept, which some days seemed to be very little. I was exhausted. For days I did not get out of my robe, shower or put on make up. When I was not Elisa's personal nursemaid, I was driven by Paco's impossible demands of a clean, orderly home and a hot meal on the table when he walked in the door. I was going crazy. With my family in New York and Paco's family in Mexico, we did not have any family in the area. The only real friend I had made at church was busy with her own infant son. We were relatively new to the neighborhood, so few neighbors even knew our names. It was a dark time punctuated with moments of clarity. Despite my depression, there were many late nights and early mornings in the nursery when I would rock Elisa to sleep and meditate on the awesomeness of God to give us such a perfect gift. Exhausting as she was, I was extremely thankful to God for her.

Because we were so worn out, we did not go to church for five weeks after Elisa was born. Finally, in early September, we felt strong enough and rested enough to go out in public with our baby girl. I do not remember much about the service. I do remember, however, how puzzled I was by the fact that some people had literally run down the aisle and kneeled at the altar, crying uncontrollably at the end of the service. Paco was the first to bring it up when we got to the van.

"Did you see how those people made fools of themselves today in church? What's that all about, anyway?" he muttered in a disgusted tone. "I can't stand to see people make spectacles of themselves. Why can't people be more private with their emotions?"

I heartily agreed.

We talked about it all of the way home and continued our discussion in the kitchen. I had been thinking about God and had decided if I was going to be a Christian, I was going to be a Christian my way. I posed my thoughts to Paco.

"I've been thinking about God," I announced, matter-of-factly. "If God really knows who I am and loves me the way I am, He'll accept me as I am. God knows how I am. He made me. I've never bowed to anything, so why should He expect me to bow to Him? I believe if He is a just and good God, He will let me enter heaven, regardless of whether I bow to him or not. I have a good heart and I have always helped old and sick people."

Paco did not argue with my logic. In fact, he did not have much to say at all. It seemed all of my lofty rhetoric was pretty much falling on deaf ears.

The next Sunday was a day like any other. We got to church on time and sat way in the back, as usual, so no one would notice us. As the preacher began his sermon, I detected something was different almost instantly. It seemed as though I was in a vacuum and the sermon was on a loudspeaker. I sat and listened intently for the first time since I had visited the church: **"You think you're gold on God's doorstep. You've been telling God how good you are and that you deserve to go to heaven. You don't even see sin in your life. You're so proud, you don't even see your sin as sin. You've desecrated God. You've fornicated. The Bible says fornicators will not enter the kingdom of God, yet you say you will enter. You believe you won't even have to bow your knee to Him. How long do you plan on running from God? At some point the hounds of heaven will stop nipping at your heels and you'll be lost in your sin forever."**

I felt as though I had just been slapped hard. My whole body was pulsating as my heart pounded wildly. God was literally speaking to me and me alone. And I knew it. My stomach sunk as I looked down at Elisa and then over to Paco. How long was I planning on putting off my decision for Christ? How soon before He would stop wooing my heart and let me slide further and further into sin?

The preacher continued with a call to the altar. "There are two people out there who God has called by name today. You know who you are. Come down to the altar and give your life to Christ right now." Then he took a long, extended pause. "I'm not in any hurry. I've got all day."

I squirmed in my seat as my conversation from the week before echoed in my ears. "I refuse to bow to God." Suddenly, that sounded like such a ludicrous statement. How could I, a mere mortal, possibly believe I would not bow to a mighty, holy God? My mind raced as my heart tried to sort out my motives. I did want to go forward and give my life to Christ, but I knew, as I examined Paco's profile, I was risking our relationship. He had made it clear that he thought all people who went forward were weak.

I looked down at our infant daughter's face, so angelic as she lay sleeping in my arms. What would her life be like if I refused to heed the call of God on my life? I shuddered to think about it. I had to go. That was all there was to it. I heard the pastor making what I feared would be his final plea. "Come on now. There are two people out there who need to come down to the altar. Just obey the voice in your heart and come to the Lord now."

I still do not know how I got the physical strength to hand Elisa over to Paco and run down the aisle.

Paco's face, bewildered and betrayed, said it all. Just as I had suspected, he was not going to take this life changing decision I had just made too well. But I did not care. I ran down the aisle and collapsed at the altar, sobbing uncontrollably. My small frame was shaking all over. At long last, my struggle with God had come to an end. I surrendered myself completely to the Lord Jesus as I repeated the sinner's prayer with the prayer minister at the railing.

When I stood to my feet and walked back to my seat, I felt as though I was walking on air. Nothing Paco could do or say to me would change the way I felt. For hours, a sense of indescribable peace and pure, unadulterated love lingered with me. I basked in the sweet savor of God's spirit, knowing that although one battle was over, another battle on a different front had just begun.

Paco was visibly angry with me. "Why did you do that?" he demanded through clenched teeth once we got in the van. "Do you have any idea how much you just embarrassed me in front of every-one back there?"

I chose to remain silent and pray for wisdom. I could only imag-ine how difficult the whole scene must have been for him. Having been raised by dignified parents in a well-to-do Mexican family, Paco was taught what others thought was extremely important.

When I did speak, I chose my words carefully. "I had to go down, honey. I can't even explain to you how it all happened. It was so supernatural. It was as though God was reading my mail. I just knew if I didn't give my life to Him today, I might never have another chance. I can only pray one day you will understand."

Wow, I could hardly believe my own ears. Was this the same woman who just a week earlier had refused to bow to God? My eyes filled with tears just thinking about the words I had spoken that day. "Please forgive me, Jesus," I prayed silently. "I didn't know what I was saying." One thing was for sure: I would never forget the bold statements I had made the week before or the repentance I felt a week later for even thinking such a thing. The stark contrast of the way I felt "before" and "after" my conversion would be etched in my mind for as long as I lived.

Everything in my life was different now that I had given my life to Christ. Every waking thought was turned over to the Lord. I prayed in earnest continually. I hardly even recognized myself when I looked in the mirror. My face had a new softness about it. I felt so much kinder and gentler in everything I said and did. I felt rested and restored physically.

I had so many questions for God. I spoke to Him as though He was sitting in a chair next to me. It felt as though I had a new best friend - and his name was God! I pinched myself every time I thought about it. I had never imagined life could be so new and exciting. Now that God was first, everything else in my life seemed to just fall into place.

Christian radio and television programming became a lifeline to me during that time. I kept it going wherever I was and filled my mind and spirit with the Word of God. There was an expectancy in my spirit that I could not explain. God was going to make every-thing in my life right – I just knew it.

As wonderful as the world looked to me, it seemed to be getting more and more dismal for Paco. We really had not prepared ourselves adequately for our loss of income when I stopped work-ing. Getting by on Paco's small salary was nearly impossible. Without a savings account to our name, it was not unusual to have less than $5.00 in our checking account from one week to the next. When we filled up our van with high priced gas, rising to almost $2.00 a gallon, I fought back tears. My only consolation was the memory of the day we bought the van from an evangelist in South Dallas. A maxi van seemed like such a neat idea for a family-to-be.

Of course, gas was not an issue then and neither was money. I was working, and gas cost significantly less.

While searching for a vehicle, I had answered an ad in the paper. That same night, Paco and I found ourselves in this traveling evangelist's home, waiting for him to bring the van out for us to see. "Have a seat," he said, directing us to sit on the worn sofa in front of the TV. "I'll be back in a minute." Since it was his house, we felt it would be rude to change the channel. So we sat for at least ten minutes and watched as two television evangelists gave "words" to the listening audience. We had never seen anything like it before. Paco and I looked at each other with skepticism. Who were these men? And how did they know what God was thinking? When the evangelist came back in the room to get us, I decided not to be shy. I had to know. "Do you know what these two guys are doing?" I asked. "We've never seen anything like this. Is what they're doing Biblical?" Looking back, I am sure we played right into his hands. At the time, we did not even think about why he would ask us to wait in front of a Christian TV program while he left us alone for ten minutes.

He seemed glad I asked. "Those two men," he explained gently, "are men of God. Their names are Pat Robertson and Ben Kinchlow and they host a show called *The 700 Club*. They are praying that the Holy Spirit will use them to show people that God is real and cares personally for them. When they have a 'word of knowledge' concerning someone's condition, they share it with their listening audience and someone who has that condition is simultaneously or gradually healed by God. It's an amazing miracle that's very hard to explain if you've never experienced it for yourself."

I thought about his explanation and decided to file it in my brain and research it later. He seemed to be sincere, as did the two men on television, but I had my reservations.

Thinking back on that evening when we bought the van seemed to dull the financial pain of the unwise vehicle purchase when I gassed up the van. I smiled thinking of how God in His sovereign way knew why He wanted our paths to cross with the evangelist months before I gave my life to Christ. I am sure we were an answer to his prayer. Quite possibly, God did something in our hearts that night as well. One thing was for sure: That would not be the last time *The 700 Club* would impact our lives. The Lord sprinkled our lives with blessings through the years from our affiliation with that program and the teachings of Pat Robertson. In many ways, he became our spiritual father and mentor, especially during the early years when we were often homebound.

One of the hardest things for Paco to bear, next to our impoverished finances, was the pressure he was feeling from me and from the church witnessing team. Everything changed once I became a Christian. I wanted to go back to church on Sunday nights, Wednesday nights and whenever the church doors opened. When I was not at church, the church would come to our house on nights when teams were sent out to witness. Paco was feeling trapped. He became so angry and bitter that I had to ask the church to stop sending people to our house to tell Paco about the Lord.

At the same time, the Lord convicted me of deserting my husband for the church. I knew that I could keep my faith by going to church once a week and by supplementing my life with Christian broadcasting. I missed the fellowship my outings brought, but it was worth the sacrifice to see Paco happy just to have me home.

The stress on our finances was more than either of us could bear. Although I had returned to work in my commission-based office furniture sales job, my sales were flat. I knew from previous experience how long it would take for my cold calls to pay off.

Frankly, we did not have the time to wait. My six-year old car was breaking down often now and we needed a miracle to be able to pay for the repairs. I took my burden to the Lord in prayer. I knew He had the answer.

One night, while Paco could watch Elisa for me, I made a bold move. "I'm going into the nursery to pray, honey. I'll be out when I have an answer from God. Will you watch her for me for as long as it takes?"

Paco shrugged his shoulders and agreed. "I guess so. Try not to take too long," he said, eyeing Elisa suspiciously. She had a history of being colicky from seven to ten at night, so I knew that was a tall order.

I had no idea how long it was going to take. I just knew that whatever it took, I was not coming out until God had given me an answer. I shut the door behind me and did not turn on a light. Somehow, the dark room seemed to bring peace to my troubled soul. I started to pray the only way I knew how. My prayer life was fairly limited. I had not yet learned how to pray the Word and I had not been given my prayer language yet, so I prayed very simple prayers. Yet I knew with all of my heart that God knew where I was and how much I needed Him, regardless of my prayer limitations.

"God, we need You now. We're at the end of our rope, Lord. Jesus, please help us. Please give me direction tonight. You know how much I need to hear from You. We're broke and need money. My car needs a new radiator. I don't know how we're going to pay for it. Please, Lord, show me now what You want me to do. I'll stay here all night if I have to, waiting for Your direction in our lives."

A still, small voice spoke to my spirit. "Do you remember the company you called on today that offered you a job? Do you remember how you told the owner, when he asked you to come to work for him, you would have to pray about it and ask God if it was His will? Why haven't you asked Me?"

I was stunned. When the man offered me a job, I told him I would pray about it and get back with him, but I did not. I had not even thought about it since. After all, I did not have any expertise in oil and gas sales. I was sure I would not excel in that field. "Do You want me to accept that job, Lord? If You do, I will. But I have to tell You that I can't even imagine myself doing well. Also, I didn't see any saleswomen there. It seemed to be all men. The owner said they all work long days and get started early. I don't know how I could possibly compete with those guys, Lord. But if You want me to go there, I will. Your will, not mine, be done."

Again the Lord spoke to my spirit in a still, small voice. "Tell them you'll work from ten in the morning to three in the afternoon, three days a week. Tell them you prayed about it and God told you to come to work for them. I will bless your efforts."

Wow. I could hardly believe what my spirit was hearing. And yet, there was not an ounce of doubt that I had heard God's voice giving me specific direction. I ran out of the nursery to tell Paco the good news. He was surprised, I think, and relieved to see me so soon.

"Honey, I heard God speak to me directly. He gave me direct

instructions to accept a job offer I got from an oil and gas exploration company today."

"Vicki, are you sure? You don't know anything about oil and gas exploration."

"Exactly! I think that is why God wants me to accept the job. So I can see how strong He is in my weakness." Paco was visibly struggling with the decision. "Honey, are you willing to believe that God just spoke to me and that He knows what's best for my life? We don't really have a better plan for our lives, do we?"

Paco nodded grudgingly. "You are right. If you believe you heard from God, who am I to argue with you? You are sure, right? Absolutely positive, right?'

I was almost jumping I was so excited.

"Yes. I am positive. God spoke to me clearly."

I still could not believe my own ears. How was it possible that God would speak to me so clearly in such a short period of time shut up in a bedroom? I tried to fathom how it all worked. How could God have time for me and care enough to make such specific recommendations to me? It all seemed so eerie and supernatural. Whatever. I never wanted to lose touch with God and with this incredible feeling that not only did He love and care for me personally, but He also had a perfect will for my life.

The next eight months were ethereal for me. My new boss seemed surprised and delighted when I accepted his offer and he was more than willing to give me the hours I asked for, considering I was strictly on commission. There were thirteen veteran salesmen in the office, working five days a week, ten hours a day. They were a fiercely competitive bunch whose main motivation was to outdo each other.

I did not have time to socialize with them much. The three days a week I worked, I went straight to my office, prayed before each phone call, worked and prayed through lunch and left at three o'clock sharp. Within weeks I made my first sale. Within months, I was the top salesperson in the office. Everyone, including me, was amazed. God was awesome. He had delivered us from our poverty and given us hope for a future. At the same time, I was honestly able to say I could not take any of the credit for my supernatural success. I gave Him all of the glory openly. I was psyched as I literally watched God in action. I still found it hard to believe that it was that easy.

Pray and obey. God would do the rest. Who knew?

God spoke to me again shortly after I accepted the job. This time I was just minding my own business. He just spoke to me out of the blue one day.

"Put your house on the market and it will sell. I will show you where I want you to move."

"Okay. This is going to be interesting," I thought. We were perfectly happy in our neighborhood. I wondered what God knew that we did not. With Paco's permission, I called a realtor immediately and we listed our house. The realtor warned us that houses in our neighborhood historically moved slowly. We were in a bad neighborhood and did not even know it. However, I refused to allow myself to get discouraged. If God said it would sell, it would sell.

In faith, Paco and I started looking for a new home. After we went through a model home tour, we felt we had found a plan that perfectly fit our contemporary tastes. We signed an offer to purchase the home, with a contingency that our house would have to sell in three months. Amazingly, the house sold quickly, and we were in our new home by early February. Things were happening so fast it was scary. It had been just four and a half months from the time I accepted the Lord. In that short period of time, we had sold our home and paid off our van with the equity. I had become the top salesperson in my organization among a group of veteran salesmen. And we owned a brand new, three-bedroom, two-bath home in a new neighborhood. We had even traded in my old car for a new family sedan. If this was any indication, we were on our way to a very exciting life. I had no idea when I gave up everything to serve God that He was going to give me exceedingly, abundantly above whatever I had asked or dreamed.

From my very first paycheck, I could not wait to write my tithe check, giving ten percent back to Him. Of all the things that broke my heart the first few months of my salvation, it was watching the offering plate being passed in front of me. I hated being empty-handed, not having anything to give God. I begged God to give me something so that I could give it back to Him. Now I couldn't wait to bless God back with a portion of what He had given me.

June was my greatest month yet. I had remained in the number one sales slot since February. I could hardly believe how good God was to us. Everyday, I thanked Him from the bottom of my heart. We took our first vacation alone together at the end of June in Acapulco. While we were there, the Lord spoke to me again.

"Quit your job. I will show you where I am sending you next." I could not believe what I was hearing. I had just made more money in one month than I had made in the entire previous year. Why would God want me to leave now?

"Why, Lord? Why would you take me away from a job that is so lucrative?" Convinced I had heard from God, I felt a strong sense of urgency to tell my boss as soon as I got back from my vacation. Just before I left town, I had won a contest that gave me a free trip for two to Las Vegas and a corner office. My boss was incredulous. He could not believe I was leaving when I was doing so well. I could not either. I just knew that I had to do what God was calling me to do. He obviously knew better than I did what the future held for me.

The month of July, I took off time to pray and visit my folks for a week in Upstate New York with Elisa. I had accepted a job with a smaller company that also explored for oil and gas wells. I would begin upon my return to Dallas. I was the only salesperson and the man that owned the company was the developer and land man. I felt good about him, and believed that God gave me peace about working for him. But I knew when I accepted the assignment it was to be for a short time. The Lord had assured me that He had something greater for me at the right time, if I would humble myself and work in a low key environment – a vivid contrast to my previous workplace. When I accepted the job, my new boss also knew it was temporary. I was completely transparent about my conversation with God and His instructions for my life. His mixed reaction didn't even bother me. I was getting used to being considered a crazy, fanatical Christian. I really did not care. I was determined to be a fool for Christ, if that meant being in the center of His perfect will.

The Lord did not take long to reward me for my obedience to Him. He totally caught me off guard, though, by His generous, extravagant gift. While I was visiting my parents' home the last week of July, I got a call from Paco.

"Vic. I have something to tell you." His voice was low and hushed, as though he was having trouble talking.

"What is it, honey? Are you all right? You sound strange."

"I feel strange, Vic. I don't know exactly what happened to me this afternoon. I've been on my knees crying with my hands lifted to the Lord. I gave Him my life today."

I was overcome with emotion. Never in my wildest dreams had I expected the Lord to touch Paco in such a way while I was gone. I had given up on believing God for a life-changing salvation experience for Paco. It had been over ten months since I had given my life to the Lord and I had learned to live with the polite tension that existed in a relationship that was not exactly evenly yoked. I could not believe my ears. While I was gone, Paco got saved! Leave it to God to touch Paco in the privacy of our own living room in my absence. I could hardly wait to get home to my new husband and life.

Once again, God had moved sovereignly in our lives, proving that His thoughts are not our thoughts and His ways are not our ways. I resolved to never again doubt His power to change lives.

In the late fall of 1980, God had another surprise in store for us. I had worked less than four months for my new employer when the Lord gave me my new marching orders. "I want you to start your own oil and gas exploration company. I'll be with you, to lead you and guide you along the way. There is nothing to fear."

"Nothing to fear," I thought. I had all kinds of fears. Although I was starting to feel like I knew something about sales, I literally was clueless when it came to forming and running a company. God knew He would have to lead me by the hand every step of the way.

"I will do it, Lord. I believe you know what is best for my life." The peace I felt as I chartered my new corporation was unexplainable. I knew God was in charge, regardless of what my future held.

Once again, my reward for obedience was almost immediate. The first week of December, I was listening to Christian radio and heard a commercial for a "Holy Spirit Forum" to be held at a Pentecostal church in Richardson. As much as I loved the people at our small Baptist church, both Paco and I knew it was time to move on in our Christian walk. We had no idea what was out there. We were still just babes in Christ. Somehow, though, we knew there was something more to learn. We had stopped growing spiritually where we were. In the back of my mind, I had not forgotten the two television evangelists that had "words of knowledge" for the audience. I wanted to experience that kind of power from God for myself.

I told Paco about the forum and asked him if he wanted to go. When he agreed, I arranged for Elisa to stay overnight with her day sitter, sensing we would not want to be rushed.

We arrived at the church at seven o'clock. There was a small crowd gathered and the presentation was about to begin. The presentation was not very long, just an hour or so, and we were free to leave. We had so many questions, we felt compelled to seek out the young couple afterward and ask them if they minded going with us for coffee. They agreed to meet us up the street. We spent the next few hours with a couple we had never met, asking questions about the Holy Spirit.

Once we felt our questions were satisfactorily answered, we left with a promise to meet them the next night at the church to experience the church service.

And what a service it was. We were completely unprepared for the strange culture of this congregation. The women, all without makeup, had long hair and wore long dresses. The men seemed equally out of touch with the 20th century. We wanted to turn and run, but it was too late. Our new friends had spotted us and were ushering us up to a reserved area in the front. I felt all of the self-consciousness I had experienced when I first attended our small church in Mesquite returning. The fear and panic were suffocating. Somehow, I managed to clear my mind of my fear and concentrate on why I was there. I knew the Lord was leading us down a path of His making. We were so new in Him and so determined to serve Him, I knew He would personally signal my spirit if anything we were about to experience was not in His perfect will. I decided to relax and let God move in my life.

I looked over at Paco. His hands were partially raised. He appeared to be concentrating on the Lord, as well. I tried to raise my hands a little. I had wanted to raise my hands in the Baptist church, but felt I would be out of place. Now, these people all had their hands raised and I could not make my body do what my mind wanted it to do. Why was it so difficult to raise my hands to God? I decided to push past the fear and obey my spirit. I raised my hands.

Immediately, my face felt flushed and there was a warming sensation over my body. I did not honestly know if it was the Lord's spirit or my own self-consciousness betraying me. I was lost in my own thoughts for some time before I was jolted by what sounded like a low roar of voices. I had never heard anything like it before. The roar started low and grew in momentum until it was loud and consumed the church. I did not dare open my eyes. What on earth were these people doing? I could not make out any single voice, but it seemed as though the whole congregation was speaking in different tongues.

I still did not open my eyes. More than anything, I wanted to see what Paco was doing. But I kept my eyes shut. Then I heard a woman's voice in my ear. It was the lady we had been with the evening before for coffee. "Vicki, it's okay. Just relax and let the Holy Spirit give you your prayer language. Relax your mouth and ask God to fill it. He will fill you with his love and a language that is all your own."

My mind was still fighting. I was not used to being in a situation where I had no control. I fought feelings of defensiveness and entrapment. Yet, I kept telling myself that God could use these people and this time in my life for His glory if I would let Him. I did as I was told and concentrated on the Lord. I was worshipping Him with my mouth saying, "Father, I adore You. You are worthy to be praised. Glory to the Lamb. Jesus is the Lamb."

Whatever came to my mind, I spoke in earnest to the Lord. For the first time in my life, I was worshipping Him in spirit and in truth.

To my disappointment, I did not get my prayer language at that time. Neither did Paco, although when they heard him praying in Spanish, someone announced that he was speaking in tongues. We looked at each other and giggled. People can be so funny. We determined not to become distressed over our inability to receive our new prayer language. In good time, we knew if God wanted that for us, He would give it to us.

The people who had gathered around us asked us if we would like to be included in the baptismal ceremony they were having in a few minutes. Although we had attended a Baptist church, neither of us had been baptized. I nodded my head "yes" and Paco followed suit. We were quickly escorted to the baptismal, and within what seemed like minutes, we were in line to be baptized. I could hardly contain the excitement in my spirit. The whole evening had become an exhilarating exaltation to the Lord. I had never really lost myself in worship like I had that evening. And now, I was going to bury my "old self" once and for all in the waters of baptism. My spirit was soaring when I went into the water. When I came out of the water, I was speaking in a new language I had never before heard and knew I could never make up. It was a glorious touch from God I would never forget.

Although we left the church around 10:00, I remained in a deep sense of awe and worship for hours. It was well past 1:00 in the morning before I fell asleep, still feeling a strong dose of God's love pulsating through my spirit.

Once again, I had entered a portal from which there was no return. That day marked the beginning of an entirely new thing God was about to do in our lives. We could not have known then how much God had in store for us. However, we were soon to find out. There were definitely some bumps up the road.

> *"...let our lives lovingly express truth [in all things, speaking truly, dealing truly, living truly]. Enfolded in love, let us grow up in every way and in all things into Him Who is the Head; [even] Christ (the Messiah, the Anointed One).*
>
> *Ephesians 4:15*

> *"And he asked them, Did you receive the Holy Spirit when you believed [on Jesus as the Christ]?"*
>
> *Acts 19:2*

CHAPTER 2

Salvation Comes To My Household

I vividly remember January 1981. I had just found out I was pregnant for our second child – a miracle, considering we had been trying to conceive for months. Amazingly, the doctors would confirm I conceived December 10th, the day after I was filled with the Holy Spirit and baptized. How like God to bring a new life into our lives at such a joyous time.

Everyday was filled with new beginnings for us. We had started attending a new, Spirit-filled church, and we were excited to be around a new group of believers. Although we missed our friends from the Baptist church, this new group of Christians seemed to be so full of hope. One of the first Sunday nights we attended, the pastor announced he felt led to try something different. Everyone was to break up into groups of three or four and find a private space in the church to pray to God for something impossible.

Paco and I looked around for our prayer partner. A man we had never met approached us and asked if we needed someone to believe with us for a miracle. We nodded and he led us off into a small chapel room, just big enough for our small group. We pulled our chairs together and formed a small circle. It was the first time I had seen this man in the light.

"His face is glowing, almost like Moses must have looked when he came down from his time with God on Mount Sinai," I thought.

To this day, I have never seen anyone, including any preacher, who had the countenance this man had. It was an awe-inspiring sight. He introduced himself and said he was a postman from Mesquite. After the small talk, he got right to business.

"What do you folks need to believe God for tonight? Think of the most impossible situation in your life, and let's ask God to move on your behalf."

I looked over at Paco. He did not seem to have anything in particular in mind. I was digging deep, trying to think of an impossible situation in our lives. My first thought was to ask God for the healing of my older brother, Robbie, retarded from birth. His healing would be considered impossible. As difficult as it had to be to live life as a retarded person, at least he was assured of a place in heaven with the Lord. He would enjoy eternal life someday, on the other side.

Then it came to me. We could pray for my parents' salvation. Now that was an impossible situation. I knew, beyond a shadow of a doubt, if God did not intervene in their lives, they were both going to go to hell when they died. My Dad was a self-described atheist and my Mom was just a hopelessly lost, church-going woman who did not want to hear anything about heaven or being born again. The few times that either my sister or I approached my parents on their need for salvation, they were so angry and defensive that we knew it was hopeless to even try to witness to them.

Dad had been an alcoholic when he was in his twenties. With the help of AA, he raised himself up out of that lifestyle to become a self-made, well-to-do businessman.

My Mom, on the other hand, had been raised by a childless couple from the age of twelve. Her dad and grandparents were too poor to keep her, so they gave her to this prosperous couple to raise for them.

My Mom and Dad had been together since they were fourteen, so the rules for their relationship were etched in stone. My Mom was Dad's "right hand" at home and in business. Whatever Dad said was gospel, as far as she was concerned. Dad pretty much dictated her views on most things, including born-again Christians. They were so indignant when I tried to witness to them on my last trip home at Thanksgiving, that I had decided I would not be trying to get home too often. It was just too painful.

"My parents' salvation," I announced firmly. I looked at Paco to see if he agreed. He did. "Can we please pray that my unsaved parents would find the Lord?" Our eyes locked as he extended his hands toward us.

"Of course. I believe with all my heart that the Lord will touch your parents immediately, that the scales will fall from their eyes, and that they will not only be saved, they will be powerfully transformed by the power of the Holy Ghost."

He proceeded to pray the most powerful prayer I had ever witnessed. His firm grip on my hand felt like fire. I could feel power literally surging from his hand into mine. It was a night I would never forget. When we left that room, I had no doubt God had heard his prayer. I felt so privileged to be in agreement with such a powerful man of God.

Oddly, we never saw him again after that night. We stayed on at that church for nearly a year. After we witnessed an incredible transformation in my parents in a short period of time, we could not help but wonder if we had prayed with an angel. God certainly moved heaven and earth to bring my parents into the kingdom almost immediately.

The following Sunday night, just one week from the night we had prayed for my parents, the phone rang. I answered it. It was my Dad. "Hey, Vic. Halleluiah! Praise the Lord."

"Dad," I reprimanded. "Stop making fun of the Lord."

"I'm not making fun, Vickum. I mean it. We've just come from an all day crusade. I have never seen so many genuine miracles in my life. We have been praising God all day."

I stood very still, trying to take in what my Dad was saying. My parents had never been to any kind of crusade in their lives. They would not be caught dead at a crusade. I could not even drag them to an hour-long church service. How could they possibly sit through a daylong crusade? My mind was reeling from the thought of it. I tried to contain my excitement. "Tell me more, Dad. How did God get you to an all day crusade?" The story that ensued was miraculous.

Two days after we had prayed, a Christian farmer had come into Dad's farm equipment dealership. "Bob," he said with conviction. "The Lord has sent me here to tell you that your time has come. God is calling you to Himself. There is an all day crusade in Rochester this Sunday. God wants you to go. He promises to answer all of your questions about Him at the crusade. He will show you miracles you never believed He could do. Will you and your wife go to the crusade on Sunday?" My Dad had told him that he would think about it and see.

Then the second Christian farmer came to visit my Dad. It was Thursday night and Dad was home alone. The farmer had a friend with him. "Bob," the farmers said. "We have come to give you a word from God."

"Come on in, boys. I have been expecting you."

Somehow, the Lord had prepared my Father for a second visitation. These two men said they had been struggling with the command the Lord had given them to stop by and give my Dad the word the Lord had for him. They finally obeyed and went to his house. My father listened for over thirty minutes as the two farmers shared with him about their own testimonies.

Before they left, they gave him this word, "My son, I have called you by name. It is time to stop fighting my Holy Spirit and come to me."

When they left, my father knew that the Sunday crusade was not an option. It was a direct command from God.

Sunday came and Mom and Dad dressed in their Sunday best to go to the crusade in the city. They were country folks and did not know what to expect when they got there. There was a huge tent outdoors filled with people. They had arrived fairly early and were able to get good seats high in the back.

When they first sat down, my Father had an idea. He saw a young boy sitting in front of him with glasses on the thickness of soda bottles. "God," he prayed. "If You are real, heal that little boy's eyes. If that little boy leaves this tent without glasses on today, I will believe that You truly exist." My Dad's excitement was contagious as he told me of how the little boy went forward to be prayed for and came back to his seat without his glasses on. "At that point,"

Dad said, "I decided we would stay until the crusade was over and the last person left."

"That's an amazing story, Dad. Thanks so much for sharing it with me. You have no idea how much that story builds my faith."

When I hung up the phone, I just stood by the phone for a minute, trying to grasp how God could move so quickly in my parents' lives. They had been so harsh and angry with me when I witnessed to them. Once again, I was reminded that God's ways are not our ways.

I also thought about the farmers that had been obedient to the unction of the Holy Spirit. Witnessing to my Dad was no small task. They knew him well. They knew he was an opinionated atheist. Yet, they loved God and my Dad enough to follow through on the directive to witness to him. I was very encouraged.

God was not through with my parents yet, though. He had much more in store for them. The following Sunday, they turned on the television on Sunday morning (something they rarely or never did) and listened to gospel music. Not realizing the music was to be followed by preaching, they sat and enjoyed the music together. At the end of the segment, Jimmy Swaggart came in front of the camera and announced that he would be starting at Genesis 1:1 and going through the Bible each week. By springtime, my parents were loyal viewers of the show. When I called to let them know that Jimmy was coming to Dallas for a crusade, my Father did not hesitate. "We will be there all three nights," he said. "We wouldn't miss seeing Jimmy for the world." I had lived in Dallas for nearly four years and my parents had only visited me once. I knew this must mean a lot to them.

My parents arrived the day before the crusade started. It dawned on me, as I listened to them talk in our living room that night, they had changed considerably. They had learned so much about the Bible in a very short period of time. I felt weak in the Word in comparison. My Mom told us about a disturbing dream she had the week before. She was in a canoe in a river. There was a waterfall that she was afraid of going over; however, she had to go over it if she was to get to the other side, where her brother, who had died when he was 19, was waiting for her. She woke up before she knew what decision she had made.

The next day came quickly, and before we knew it, we were filing into the huge auditorium for the crusade. I learned from my Mom that she had been in touch with the Jimmy Swaggart crusade team and had arranged to meet Jimmy backstage one night during the crusades. My parents had become faithful givers and responded to nearly every appeal Jimmy made during the time they had been watching the show. They had a gift they wanted to give him personally. I wanted to pinch myself to be sure I was not dreaming. I had never, in my wildest dreams, imagined that my parents' belligerent attitude toward the Lord could be so changed. It reminded me of my own conversion to Christ.

That night, June 19, 1981, my Father accepted the Lord in a Jimmy Swaggart crusade. Two days later, my Mother went forward to accept the Lord. The evening before, we had gone backstage with one of the team members to meet and greet Jimmy personally. The four of us were alone with him for a few minutes. I left with the Bible he preached from the previous evening.

Before we left, he asked me if he could lay hands on my womb and pray for my unborn child, Jessica. As he prayed over my womb, I thanked Jesus for all He had done in our lives, in my parents' lives, and for what He would someday do in our children's lives.

As we drove away from leaving my parents at the airport the following day, I felt so blessed. "God is so good," I thought. I had never experienced a more exciting, fulfilling weekend with my Mom and Dad. I never thought I would have the privilege of actually being with my parents when they came to the Lord.

When my parents arrived home, they were indeed changed people. My sister, Marcia, swears she did not recognize them as they walked up the sidewalk to her front door. They were so transformed. I have noticed since how few new converts are as "on fire for the Lord" as my parents were when they accepted Christ.

My oldest sister, Luanne, was downright angry with them. She felt betrayed. In her words, "My parents went to Dallas and never came back. The people who returned were people I had never met before."

When business owners in a small town come to the Lord, they

have a definite circle of influence. If you think about it, a small town is a captive audience: They are not going anywhere, anytime soon.

Actually, a number of people in town were upset with my parents. The Methodist preacher and his wife were especially hurt at my Mom's insistence that she could not stay in a church where the preacher did not believe it was necessary to be born again. She and Dad spent hours with them, teaching them from the book of John that Jesus instructed Nicodemus, a religious man, to be born again. But it was to no avail. Although everyone was watching, few people were willing to listen. No one wanted to give up his old ways.

A few months later, the phone rang late on a Friday night. It was my sister Luanne. "I'm saved!" she cried into the phone. "I'm saved! I'm saved!" I was startled. My first thought was that she was mocking me. It took me a minute to respond.

"Luanne," I said softly, "are you making fun of me?" It seemed to me to be a rather cruel trick. She did not hesitate in her response.

"Vicki, I gave my life to Christ in church tonight. I am born again!"

How amazing is that? If my parents were tough, Luanne was tougher. She had told me, in no uncertain terms, that if I ever mentioned Jesus and the plan of salvation to her kids again, I would not be allowed near them. When I talked to them about the Lord the night I babysat them (they were 10,11 and 12), she asked me to leave, she was so irritated with me.

She had also been a faithful member of the local Methodist church. And now she was a child of the King. I could hardly contain my happiness for her. "Luanne, I am so thrilled for you. God is so awesome. Your life will never be the same." And it never was.

The next morning, at 7:46 a.m., Jessica Anne was born in the privacy of our bedroom at home with the help of Paco and our midwife. We praised God for a quick and safe delivery, since I gave birth within ten minutes of the time the midwife arrived.

Every year, the day before Jessica's birthday, I think of Luanne and am reminded of God's sovereign work in her life. It was not long – just a matter of days, actually – that Luanne's husband also gave his heart to Christ. To this day, they are strong in the Lord and serving God.

Just two months after Luanne and Cliff's conversions to Christ, I had another major paradigm shift in my life. Once again, the Lord took me completely by surprise. Paco and I flew up to New York to visit our folks with our two little girls. We were anxious to attend their new church and dedicate Jessica to the Lord in the presence of my family members and friends. Ironically, the day was Sunday, October 31st – Halloween Day.

After the dedication service, there was a potluck meal in the basement of the church. After the potluck, the pastor encouraged our family to stay for a time of prayer. My sister, Marcia, was there with her husband, Ray. They were actually the first two to come to the Lord in our family.

As Mom and Dad, Luanne and Cliff, Paco and I, and Marcia and Ray all gathered around in a circle to pray, I purveyed the room, thinking what a miracle it was that we were all standing together in a church, born-again Christians every one. I was only two years old in the Lord and everyone else, other than Marcia and Ray, were younger in the Lord than I was. We had all taken a similar path after our salvation. Each one of us was spirit-filled.

The pastor directed Ray, my brother-in-law, to sit in a chair in the middle of the circle. The rest of us held hands in a circle around Ray. Prepared for prayer, I had my head bowed and my eyes were squeezed tightly shut. The pastor spoke to me at that point and told me to open my eyes. He assured me I would want to watch the miracle God was about to perform.

I opened my eyes and watched intently. Ray was severely bow-legged. The pastor anointed Ray's head with oil and placed his hands on Ray's legs. Instead of praying, the pastor commanded Ray's body to line up with the Word of God in the name of Jesus. To my astonishment, I watched as Ray's legs obeyed the command. The muscles, tendons and bones were moving and popping into place. I could see and hear his legs being healed. It was a defining moment for me. Of all of the people in the room that day, including Ray, I was the most affected by his healing. I do not know why, but I was never the same again. The thought of that miracle still makes shivers run up and down my spine.

That evening, Paco and I had planned a date with an old friend of mine from school. She was living in the area and wanted us to meet her new boyfriend. As we prepared to go out that evening, I could not stop thinking about what I had seen that day in the church basement. I had heard of healing miracles, but I had never witnessed a healing. To see Ray stand up, taller and straighter than when he had first sat down, was amazing to me. I just could not fathom how that could happen.

We all walked into a small bar in a nearby town and sat down at a table for four. Each of us ordered a beer. I lit up a cigarette and took a deep drag on it. Although I had struggled with alcohol and cigarettes since coming to Christ, I had been unable to quit either successfully. They seemed to go hand in hand. I knew when I quit one, the other would have to go, as well. On this particular evening, neither one tasted as good as usual. Even the small talk we made around the table seemed silly and trite.

Everything felt different to me, now that I had actually witnessed a miracle. I am sure I did not look any different on the outside, but inside I was definitely a changed individual. That day, I had seen God's power in a way I had never seen it.

The next Sunday night, at home in Dallas, I was watching Jimmy Swaggart on the television in my bedroom. Suddenly, he turned his body from the camera and looked into the other camera. With pointed finger, he looked at me with a piercing glaze and said, "You carnal Christian. You say you love God, yet you go to the bar with your friends and you drink alcohol and smoke cigarettes. The Lord is a Holy God. If you want to serve God, you must be holy. The Lord is saying to give your vices to Him. He will take away your craving for alcohol and nicotine, if you will turn it all over to Him."

My heart felt like it had stopped. I knew he was talking to me. The time had finally come to put away the things of the world and serve God with all of my body and my being. The Bible says you cannot serve God and mammon. The Lord had been merciful to me. Yet, I knew it was just a matter of time before I would be lured back into the world if I did not slam the door shut on the sins that beset me. I gave my vices to God.

"Please, Lord, you know I cannot do this by myself. You know how weak I am in my flesh. Please take my desire to drink alcohol and smoke cigarettes away right now. I want to serve You with all my heart."

I praise God that I never turned back to my old life in the world. God in His mercy and grace gave me the strength every day over two decades to remain free from those addictive habits. I had tried to quit on my own and could not. I truly recognized the depth of God's love for me. He had given me a miraculous deliverance from alcohol and cigarettes.

1982 was to become forever etched in our hearts as a tremendous year of testing. I do not understand how some years are so good and some years are so bad. I can only speculate that God in His wisdom knew what we needed to build character and intensity in our lives. For us, there has not been a year like it, before or since.

Early in the year, I discovered I was pregnant. Elisa was two and Jessica was just four months old when I realized I was to bear yet another child. Incredulous with the news, I sought the Lord in earnest prayer. I was distraught with the idea of having three children under the age of three years old. I struggled with the fact that I knew God had directed me to start an oil and gas exploration business. However, I did not know how on earth I was ever going to be effective as a businesswoman or as a mother with so much going on in my life.

I had been praying since I had received the news of my pregnancy, but had not received a clear word from the Lord as to what He was planning for this next step in our lives. One morning, I opened my Bible to a special verse that really jumped out at me.

I read in Judges about the angel of the Lord appearing to Sampson's parents. They were told he was to be a special boy, a Nazarite. The angel instructed his mother not to eat or drink any unclean thing. The Lord spoke to me with a clarity I will never forget. He said, "The special child you are carrying is a son. I do not want you to eat or drink any unclean thing through this pregnancy. This child, like Sampson, will be a Nazarite, as well."

I laid my hands on my womb and meditated on the word I had received from God. "A Nazarite. I wonder what that means?"

From that day forward, I had a new bounce in my step and joy in my heart. We were going to have a baby boy! I could not even imagine what it would be like to have a son. I wondered how different it would be from having a daughter. I loved our two daughters with all of my heart.

Yet, the Lord had promised me this was not just any son. This son would be special. I knew God would give me the strength to be extra careful to eat well and take good care of my body. When I finally did go in for a sonogram, the film showed that I had conceived our son the day I quit smoking and drinking. Since I was twenty-four weeks pregnant, the radiologist asked me if I would like to know the baby's gender. When she told us it was a girl, Paco and I both answered her in unison: "It's a boy." We clung to the word the Lord had given me concerning our son. We knew this child would prove to be very special.

> *"...believe in the Lord Jesus Christ [give yourself up to Him, take yourself out of your own keeping and entrust yourself into His keeping] and you will be saved [and this applies both to] you and your household as well. And they declared the Word of the Lord [the doctrine concerning the attainment through Christ of eternal salvation in the kingdom of God] to him and to all who were in his house."*
>
> *Acts 16: 31,32*

CHAPTER 3

The House That Would Not Burn

❧

In July of 1982, the heat was unbearable. Just weeks away from delivery, I prayed daily that God would deliver me from the suffocating heat of the summer. One night, as Paco and I sat on our sofa studying the Word of God, the phone rang. It was my Dad. "Vic," Dad said. I was startled to have him calling so late at night. It was after 10:30 in Dallas and an hour later in New York. "I've been sitting here fighting God on something all night. I decided I could not go to bed tonight without calling you."

"What is it, Dad?" I asked, holding my breath.

"Well," Dad started out hesitantly, "Vic, the Lord has been showing me that you and Paco have to go to every window and door of your home tonight and anoint it with oil. I don't know why, but I am positive I heard from God. Then pray for angels to protect your home tonight. Will you do it? Promise me you will."

"Of course we will, Dad. We will do it right now. I promise."

As I hung up with my Father, I had a witness in my spirit that this was important. Although it was late and we were tired, we took the call very seriously. The only oil we could find in our cupboards was vegetable oil, so I got it out.

"Do you think this will work, honey?" I asked Paco as I poured some of the oil into the cap. Paco shrugged his shoulders and looked at me questioningly.

"I guess so. Oil is oil, right?"

I did not really know. As I thought about it, I decided it probably did not matter. At least, I hoped not.

We had never anointed our home before and we had not been with anyone else who had done it. As we went from window to window, praying in English and in the spirit, we lost total track of time. Nearly two and a half hours later, we were finished. We turned to each other and took hands. Standing by the bed, we began to pray fervently for one another. Both of us were so overcome by the power and love of the Holy Spirit, we had to sit down. We were drunk in the Spirit. It was an unusually moving experience.

The next morning, we awoke as usual and scurried around the house, getting ready for work and preparing the two girls to go to their daycare. It was storming heavily as we left the house. The storms continued on and off all morning, with periods of heavy thunder and lightning. When I returned to my office from lunch, there was a message to call my girlfriend, Charlotte.

As I hung up with her, I was shaking.

"Honey," Paco said with concern. His voice dropped to a low whisper. "What happened?" I turned around slowly and sat down.

"This is the strangest story, honey. Are you ready for this?" Paco just looked at me, a hint of trepidation in his eyes.

"I don't know. Am I?"

Paco listened in awe as I recounted the story I had just heard on the phone. According to Charlotte, a fire had broken out at our house around 10:00 that morning. Although 80 percent of our house was brick, the fire started in the air conditioning unit, which was situated next to the section of the house that was made from wood. Because we lived on a cul-de-sac of professionals, no one was around to detect the fire.

Miraculously, a stranger had driven down our street and seen the fire and reported it to the fire department. By the time Charlotte was notified, tall flames were licking the wood, but it was not burning. There were not even any singe marks or any other evidence of a fire on the wood. Charlotte said a small crowd had gathered from the neighborhood. They all watched in amazement as they witnessed the flames grow in intensity, with no damage whatsoever to our home.

After I told Paco the story, we sat looking at each other in disbelief. Paco broke the silence. "Just think, Vic. If your dad had not called and if we had not obeyed and anointed our home last night, our house could have gone up in flames today."

"I know, sweetie. I can't even imagine how different this day might have been for us. The Lord is so good. He knew what was going to happen and he intervened to save us from destruction. Doesn't it just boggle your mind? Just think, Paco: The air conditioner was next to the window where Jessica's crib is in the girl's bedroom!"

We shuddered to think if the lightning had struck our air conditioner at night. If we were not under the divine protection of a loving God, flames would have most likely consumed both of our girls before we even knew there was a fire in our house.

When the insurance adjuster came to our house and saw the huge hole the lightning bolt had created in the air conditioning blade, he just shook his head in amazement. "I have got to tell you, ma'am," he drawled in a thick Texan accent. "I have been in this business a long time. I can't say I have ever seen anything like this. I have seen a lot of bizarre things, but I have never seen lightning strike an air conditioner and leave a four-inch hole in the blade. This is the darndest thing I have ever seen."

In the summer heat, I felt cold. It would not be the last time I felt singled out by God.

> *"...the king's counselors gathered around together and saw these men - that the fire had no power upon their bodies, nor was the hair of their head singed; neither were their garments scorched or changed in color or condition, nor had even the smell of smoke clung to them. Then Nebuchadnezzar said, Blessed be the God of Shadrach, Meshach and Abednego, Who has sent His angel and delivered His servants who believed in, trusted in and relied upon Him!..."*
> *Daniel 3: 27,28*

CHAPTER 4

A Baby Nazarite's Mission From God

❧

Paco had started his own business as a freelance graphic designer and illustrator in 1981. And, of course, that year I started my oil and gas exploration company, as well. With no set income from either of us, two babies and another one on the way, 1982 was a scary year financially. Both of our businesses were in the start up stage and neither was taking off too quickly.

We could not afford health insurance and were having our babies at home with a midwife to cut down on the cost of the birth. In addition to the lowered costs, I enjoyed having my babies in the privacy of our own home with a midwife present while Paco assisted. It was a stark contrast to the nightmarish experience we had with Elisa's hospital birth.

Two days after Elisa's third birthday, our son was born. We named him Paquito, which means little Paco in Spanish. He was actually Francisco Garza IV. There were several miracles associated with his birth. The first miracle, of course, was he was male. The radiologist had insisted she had a clear view of the baby and I was carrying a girl. The second miracle was the miraculous unwrapping of the umbilical cord from his neck when he was born. The cord was wrapped tightly around his neck. As the midwife was struggling to get something to cut the cord with, it miraculously unwrapped itself.

Paco and I could not have been happier. We had a beautiful, healthy boy. Our little family was complete.

The six weeks following his birth, life was a blur. If I thought life was hectic after having my first child, having three under the age of three was a whirlwind. Simple tasks like grocery shopping were impossible. Until Paco came home to help, I was homebound with the babies. Although I tried to work from home, my business was going to have to wait. My infant and toddlers took up my every waking moment.

To make matters worse, our finances had not made a comeback. Our cash reserves were dangerously low with no income to speak of in sight. As Paco and I discussed ways to dig ourselves out of the financial pit, we both felt oppression hovering over our lives. I was the first to put my finger on it.

"It's as though we are under a curse, Paco. It feels like there is a dark cloud hanging over our lives."

Paco agreed. Every time we thought we were getting a little ahead, we would just fall farther behind.

The following week, I met a girlfriend from church to let the children play together at McDonalds. My friend and her husband had a tract ministry, so she actively sought out candidates for new Christians in her apartment complex. On this day, she had brought a neighbor from her apartment complex to McDonalds to meet me. As we sat around the picnic table watching the children, the topic quickly changed from kids to the Lord.

Janie, my friend, was telling her new neighbor about the Lord and how important it was to have unwavering faith in God, no matter what the circumstances. She prompted me to back her up on her point. I responded to her prompting with some very strong statements of faith.

Janie and I had clicked with each other from the moment we met at church. She had a way of bringing out the best in me, especially when it came to faith. Her faith had built my faith to a point where I could say to her friend with conviction, "I believe God can do anything. Not only can He do anything, I believe He is searching the earth looking for those who will believe Him for miracles."

I looked down at my infant son and made a bold statement. "I believe with all of my heart that God not only heals today, He can raise the dead." She latched onto my statement and pressed me further.

"Are you saying if your son died, God would raise him from the dead?" I nodded my head resolutely. "I believe it with every fiber of my being."

"Wow," she said. "You really do have faith."

That was on Tuesday. Thursday night, we went to the Bible study we had started to attend in a friend's home. Janie and her husband were there, as well as quite a few other couples from our church. Just before the Bible study ended, the leaders called Paco and me to the front.

They had a word from the Lord for us. "My children, I have need of you. I have called you to Myself and set you aside for a special purpose. There will be difficult days ahead for you. However, I will sustain you. Do not grow weary in well doing. You shall reap in due time if you do not faint."

We stood there, with our hands lifted high, praising God. We had known God had a special purpose for our lives and this prophecy confirmed what He had already spoken privately and personally to our spirits. However, we did not understand exactly what the Lord meant by the end of the prophecy when He assured us He would sustain us.

I had always been fairly strong. I could not imagine what we could go through that God would have to carry us through. I was about to find out.

Sometime in the wee hours of the morning, I had a horrific dream. I did not usually have nightmares. However, on this particular morning, I sat straight up in bed, the dream had been so dark and disturbing. I dreamt I was in our compact car, going around and around a steep mountain in the rain. There was no moonlight to guide me and it was pitch dark. There were no guardrails to keep my car from plunging over the mountainside if I did not stay on the road.

I was praying under my breath, trying to concentrate and stay focused on the road ahead of me, although it really felt like I was driving through a dark maze. I could only see six inches ahead of me. My hands were gripping the steering wheel with fear. When it seemed the intensity of my fear could not be greater, the car slowed to a stop. Terror gripped my soul, as I glanced down at the fuel tank. It was empty. Helplessness and terrifying fear took a hold of me as I screamed, "Jesus. Help me. Jesus! Jesus! I need you. Lord Jesus!"

Then I woke up with a start. My racing heart took time to subside. I lay in bed for quite awhile, trying to pull myself together and calm my fears. "What is it, Lord? Why do I feel such a panic wave surging over my spirit?"

Finally, I fell asleep, praying that God would help me through whatever it was I was about to experience. At the age of 26, I could not remember ever dreaming such a foreboding nightmare.

When I awoke, morning had come quickly. My spirit was still troubled. As I drove into work, I prayed in the spirit, trying to decipher what my spirit was sensing. I felt a creeping dread I could not explain.

For the first time in my Christian life, my prayer took on a different form. Transformed in the spirit, I began to pray with groaning and utterances that I had never heard come from my mouth or anyone else's. The pain I felt as I groaned in the spirit can only be likened to the beginnings of childbirth. I felt as though I was actually laboring in the spirit. Although the grieving in the spirit finally subsided, I was still not at peace.

Over lunch, I tried to tell Paco what I was experiencing. It was as though there was a suffocating cloak of evil lurking in our midst. I could sense it so strongly I could almost taste it.

That night as I watched Paco swing on the patio swing with our three children, I was still praying through what I had been feeling all day. As I washed the dishes and prayed, I felt a strong truth emerge from the void I was feeling. I ran to the patio doors in the kitchen and quickly slid them open.

"Paco!" I said with a sense of urgency. "Honey, I think I know what's happening. We need to go through deliverance in order for the curses to be broken over our lives. Are you willing to go somewhere to get prayer tonight or have someone come over here to pray for us?"

Paco agreed to a prayer meeting and I set about looking for

someone to pray over us. I called Janie and asked her for the telephone number of the prayer ministers from our church. She informed me they were on vacation and were not due back into town until the following week. Paco and I decided the prayer meeting would have to wait.

That night, I got the girls into their beds, and then I laid Paquito down on our bed to change him into his pajamas. Looking over the various sleepers I had borrowed from friends, I chose the one sleeper that belonged to him. It was a sweet terry cloth sleeper with the words "Jesus loves me" embroidered on one side. As I laid him down in his bassinet by our bed, I held him tight. "Jesus does love you, sweetie. And so do I." I crawled into bed and prayed for a good night's sleep. I was exhausted from the night before and the events of the day. Sleep came quickly.

At 5:02 a.m., I awoke with a silent alarm ringing in my spirit. I had heard Paquito crying a few minutes earlier, but now he was silent. He did not usually sleep through the night. I lay in bed, exhausted, waiting to see if he would cry again. I held my breath, praying that he would sleep though the night so I could get some rest.

For the first time since I had become a mother, the thought entered my mind that my son had died of crib death. "I bind you, Satan, in the name of Jesus," I commanded under my breath. "You have no power over my mind in the name of Jesus." I fell back asleep.

I awoke to Paco scurrying around the bedroom in the early morning light looking for his socks and shoes. "I'm getting ready to go to my Bible study with the guys, honey. I'll be back in a few hours."

I looked at the clock. It was almost 7:30.

"Wow, honey, I can't believe it. Pacquito slept all night last night."

Even as I spoke it, my relief had turned to concern.

"Honey, would you check him and make sure he is alright?" Paco leaned over the bassinet and nudged the baby. Then he looked at me with a look of horror I will never forget. Our seven-week old son had died in his sleep.

From that moment on, our entire world changed in an instant. It was as though someone was filming our lives in slow motion and we were watching from a distance. Paco immediately whisked the baby to the bed and began breathing into his mouth to try to resuscitate him.

I grabbed my bathrobe and ran out the back door and down the alley to the home of a man that I knew was a doctor. I ran through his back yard to his kitchen window, where he was making breakfast for his young children. Through the glass, I yelled, "Please come quickly. Our baby is dead!"

Within minutes, he was in our home. He had called the ambulance before he came and it arrived quickly. Paco jumped into the ambulance with the baby and the doctor and the ambulance sped away.

At the same time, the doctor's wife had come to get our two daughters to take them to their home for the day. Jessica was just thirteen months old and Elisa was three. As she was being led out the backdoor of our home, she looked at me in disbelief and asked, "Mommy, our baby is dead?" I just hugged her hard and reassured her everything would be okay. My heart broke for her, as I thought of how she had mothered him since his birth. She was a huge help, holding him and rocking him, as though he was her own. How was she ever going to recover from this?

How were we ever going to be the same again? It felt as though someone had plunged a knife deep into my heart.

Alone in the house, I tried to collect my thoughts. I called my parents. My Mom answered. "Mom!" I cried into the phone. "Paquito is dead! He died in his sleep last night."

My Mom was incredulous. "Vicki, are you sure? Are you sure you can't get him breathing again?"

My pain was apparent, I am sure, as I assured her he had been dead awhile. When I hung up the phone, I called Janie. She was as angry at the Satanic attack on our family as she was upset by the news of his death. We had spent quite a bit of time together since his birth, and she knew how difficult the year had already been for us financially.

"Vicki," she said with authority. "Jesus can raise your son from the dead. Jerry and I will believe with you for that miracle. We'll be there as soon as we can. Wait for us and we will go to the hospital together with you."

For the first time since I had awakened, I felt a glimmer of hope. I called our pastor and his wife and asked them to believe with us for our son to be raised from the dead. Although he had famous in-laws who had witnessed such miracles and written books about those kinds of miracles, he did not seem at all convinced. As I hung up the phone with him, I wondered how he could preach about these types of miracles in his sermons, yet seem so unbelieving in a real life situation. My conversation with him had been confusing and disturbing. I tried to push it out of my mind and concentrate on the Word of God.

What did Jesus say about this? He had raised Lazarus from the dead several days after he had died. Surely, He could raise up my son within hours of his death.

The wait for Jerry and Janie to come get me was excruciating. I longed to be with my baby and hold his body next to mine one last time. Although I had prayed over him quickly and asked the Lord to raise him back to life before he was taken away, I needed more time with him. My arms ached to hold him.

I prayed in the spirit for a good twenty minutes, waiting for Jerry and Janie to come. Finally they appeared, and we quickly arrived at the hospital. We ran breathlessly into the emergency room, feeling an urgency to pray over the baby before any more time passed.

Paco and our neighbor were standing outside one of the rooms. Paco was crying and said the hospital had allowed him to call his family in Mexico to tell them of our son's death. I was feeling stronger now that I was with Jerry and Janie, and told Paco with confidence, "Honey, I'm positive the Lord has allowed this in our life to test our faith. Do you believe that Jesus can raise our son from the dead? I do and so do Janie and Jerry. Let's pray over him right now and believe God for a miracle."

I saw a glimmer of hope come across his countenance. He moved past me to the emergency room personnel.

"Can you give us some time in the room with our baby? We want to pray over him." The nurse nodded compassionately. "Of course, Mr. Garza. Take as long as you need." Together, the four of us burst into the hospital room with an expectant urgency. If ever four people were in agreement, we were.

We stood over our dead son's body and laid hands on him, massaging him, commanding his body to line up with the pure and perfect will and Word of God. We pleaded with the Lord to raise him from the dead. We called him forth, commanding him to live. Our faith did not waver.

Each of us stood in complete agreement, believing with every ounce of our being that the God of the universe was well aware of our prayers and standing by to answer them.

I reminded the Lord of his promises about our son. The Lord Himself had told me that this child was to be a special child, a Nazarite. I cried out to the Lord in my faith, believing this death had occurred to bring glory to my God. I knew that few people would ever believe with the measure of faith we had for a miracle of such proportions. I begged God to use this situation to bring glory to Him.

Suddenly, our pastor burst into the room. "Put him down now," he said emphatically. "I have ordered the hospital to send the body to the morgue. Your time is up here." I just looked at him, incredulous.

"Bob," I said with fervor, "if this was your son, wouldn't you believe God to raise him up from the dead?"

"Vicki," he said with authority, "your son was born to die. I knew your son was going to die. The Lord is going to give you other sons."

"I don't want other sons," I screamed. "I want this son! How can you be so cruel?"

The nurse came into the room at that time and said, "I'm sorry, Mrs. Garza. We need this room now. You will have to leave."

I looked at Paco, Janie and Jerry, then down at our son. All of a sudden, I felt powerless. It was not fair. How could it all be over just like that? I still was not convinced that God would allow our son to die, never to be seen alive again. I looked at our pastor.

"You cannot stop God, Bob, from what He has ordained. I believe God will raise our son from the dead, whether it is today, tomorrow or the next day. God is able to move beyond the circumstances to do whatever He wants."

As we drove away from the hospital without our baby, I fought tears. Yet I refused to cry. I refused to believe this was the end of the story. I knew I had heard from God concerning the special call on our son's life. He had intervened at his birth to save him for a purpose. I was positive that purpose was to raise him from the dead, to show His glory on the earth.

Almost as soon as we walked in the door of our home, our phone was ringing. Brother, sisters, cousins, friends all called to give us their condolences. The doorbell started to ring and neighbors we hardly knew were standing in our living room, hugging us and asking if there was anything they could do.

As this flood of sympathy entered our lives, I never wanted to be more alone in my life. Paco's parents would be flying in later that afternoon to be with us and I just wanted some time to sort through what had happened. Paco was grieving visibly. Gut wrenching sobs were coming from our bedroom as he dealt with the reality that the son we had loved and nurtured was never coming back.

I, on the other hand, was empowered with the faith that I knew my God. He loved me and Paco and our family and He would not allow this type of tragedy without a reason. There had to be a reason. Every fiber of my being believed that reason was to glorify Him through our son's life being raised up once more. I refused to give up hope.

Understandably, there was a growing concern among our family, friends and neighbors that I was in denial and shock. I knew how they could think I was delusional. I did not blame them at all, knowing I would probably feel the same way if I witnessed a woman whose son had just died, saying he was going to be raised from the dead.

Somehow, though, I could not give up hope. I called Janie and asked her if there was someone else she knew from our church that could break the oppression we felt over our lives. I still felt the dark cloud hanging over our family and knew it needed to be removed before anything edifying could happen. She called me back with the name of a couple that had assisted the other deliverance ministers she knew. The four of them would stop by our house after lunch to take us through a time of prayer to break the curses.

Paco went first. Then it was my turn.

"Lay down on the floor, Vicki, and relax. Just breathe deep and keep your mouth open. Close your eyes now while I pray with you. There is nothing to be afraid of. Do not think about anything and do not try to speak or pray."

I had been praying under my breath all day, and it was hard to stop and think of nothing. Everything in me wanted to praise God, as I waited expectantly for Him to show up on the scene and reverse the events of the day.

Obediently, I did as I was told, and cleared my mind of everything. I did not want to do anything to obstruct the miracles I believed God was about to perform. As Gene held his Bible over my body and commanded all generational curses to be broken over my life, I felt as though I was slipping into another world. Although I vividly remember everything that took place during the deliverance ceremony, it was as though I was witnessing the event from outside of my body.

That single event was one of the most powerful moves of God I had ever personally experienced. My body writhed and contorted in ways I could not have imagined. The demons spoke through my body in voices I knew were not my own. A full hour later, I lay on the floor, exhausted from the experience.

When I found the strength to get up, it was as though it was the first day of my life. Everything looked different. Colors were more vivid. The Word of God seemed to literally jump off of the page at me when I read the scriptures. I ran to the bathroom and turned on the shower. As the hot water hit my body, I felt as though the Lord Himself was pouring liquid love and power into my spirit. I prayed in the spirit like never before. I was totally transformed. I was free.

When I had dressed and returned to the living room, the others were waiting for me.

"How do you feel, Vicki?"

"Absolutely unbelievably renewed. I have never felt like this. I feel like someone cleaned me from the inside out and I am totally pure. Wow, I don't know what to say. I had no idea that praying for deliverance would be such a freeing experience."

As we all sat talking in our living room about the day's events, we built one another up in faith. After a few minutes, Jerry and Janie looked at each other. "We believe that nothing is too great for God. Let's go to the morgue and lay hands on your son. Time is not an issue with God. He is not limited by time."

We all agreed and the six of us drove together to the city morgue. As we walked into the lobby, the guard was obviously taken by surprise. "You want to go down to the morgue and pray over a dead child? I guess that would be okay. I don't think anyone has ever asked to do that before. Why don't the ladies stay here in the lobby and wait while I take the men downstairs?"

The drive home from the morgue was painful. I could not believe that God still had not honored our faith. I had totally expected to be driving home with our beautiful, living son in my arms. When we got home, I called a friend who was in the funeral business. He was actually an investor with my company, so I did not know much about his faith. He agreed to pick up our son from the morgue.

The others left, also disappointed that God had not moved. Before long, Jim was in our home asking me for an outfit for the baby's burial. I went to the closet and pulled out a beautiful light blue knit overall outfit that my girlfriend Charlotte had given us when Pacquito was born. He had never worn it. I was saving it for a special occasion. When I gave it to Jim, I asked him a few questions about how he was going to pick the baby up and when he was going to dress him. It was still hard for my motherly instincts not to worry about him being cold. The lines between reality, faith and denial were blurring. I was feeling confused, and suddenly, terribly lonely.

As difficult as the next few days were, I felt an incredible shield of God's love around me. I was fasting and praying in the spirit almost around the clock. Paco's parents had flown in from Mexico and were staying with us. They were taking their grandson's death very hard. It was difficult for them to understand how I could have any hope.

I brought out the Bible and read to them from the book of John about the raising of Lazarus from the dead. I still believed it was altogether possible that the Lord had a miracle in store for our family. However, as the hours ticked away, it was becoming harder and harder for me to hold onto any hope for my miracle. With all of the decisions that had to be made concerning viewing hours, coffin choices and funeral times, I felt as though I was caught between two worlds. I had not shed a tear the day of his death, I was so focused on God and the miracle that He had in store for our family.

When I awoke the next morning, there was a dread settling into my spirit that spread an ominous dark shadow over my soul and emotions. I cried almost continually, as I tried to grasp the reality of the situation. Paco and I were both groping to hold onto our faith. There were so many questions. How could God allow our son to die? Why did He even give him to us in the first place if He was going to take him away from us? If God loved us, as we believed He did, how could He ordain such a cruel event? Why did He give us the scripture before his birth, telling us he was to be a Nazarite and a very special child? I finally decided that I needed to continue in prayer and fasting. The alternative of living "in the moment" was way too painful.

Somehow we got through the viewing hours that evening and made it through to the next morning, the day of his funeral. Although the funeral was not scheduled until early afternoon, we met with faith-filled friends at nine to pray over Paquito's body and beg God for the impossible. A handful of us met for communion at the funeral home, and then proceeded to pray in the spirit in agreement for our son's raising. I tried not to let the fact that he had been embalmed bother me. If Jesus could turn the water into wine, surely he could turn our son's embalming fluid into blood.

For nearly four hours, our little band of faithful friends prayed over our son's body. Paco's parents watched from the sidelines, horrified. They could not even imagine with what kind of a cult we were involved. It was extremely hard for his parents and the funeral director and his wife to grasp what we thought we could accomplish by this intense time of prayer.

Finally, as the hour approached for the funeral, Paco stopped the group. "I have to tell you all," he said with an overtone of resignation in his voice, "I've had a vision this morning of my son with the Lord. Jesus was holding our son in His arms and Paquito was waving goodbye to me. I know, beyond a shadow of a doubt, our son is with the Lord. I believe that vision was a sign to me to release my son to the Lord. Let's all break for now and reconvene at the funeral at 2:00."

My heart sunk. I could not bring myself to give up just yet. I knew the Lord could do anything. In my innermost spirit, I knew that regardless of what Paco had seen or thought he had seen, the Lord could move. I continued to believe.

As the cars came and the people all drew together for the graveside service, I looked around at the array of people that had congregated for our son's final goodbye. Silently, I begged God to show each one of these people how real He was and that He had no limitations to His power. We had asked our friend Jerry, an ordained minister, to lead the service. He and Janie, along with about five others, had stood by us as we believed that God could raise our son from the dead.

He gathered the group together in a circle and we all prayed for one last time that God would show up on the scene. After the group sang a song, Paco laid a verse of scripture from Isaiah on Paquito's body and the coffin was closed. Quietly, the group dispersed. The service was over. I stood in disbelief as the coffin was lowered into the ground. The pain was too intense. I could not bear it. The only one left standing beside me after the others left was Paco's Dad. I buried my head in his chest and sobbed the deepest tears I have ever cried. "No, no, no," I screamed as I clutched his shirt and cried. "It wasn't supposed to be like this!" I wanted to curl up in a ball and die. I had never felt such pain in my life.

That night at home, still more people stopped by the house to bring dinner and pay their condolences. Although I was grief-stricken and heart broken, I felt as though the events of that weekend had altered my life forever. Where I had once been a "closet Christian," I was emboldened to speak to each person that came into our house with a new intensity and power I had never felt before. My heart was broken beyond description, but my spirit was stoked with a new flame of conviction and perseverance to serve God no matter what. If Satan thought his attack on our home and family was going to stop me, he underestimated my fervor for the Lord. Now that our son was in heaven with the Lord, I felt a renewed desire to be in Heaven for eternity. I was going to serve

God no matter what the cost.

A flight attendant from our church stopped by that evening with a casserole for our dinner. Although I vaguely remembered meeting her at one of our services, I did not even know her name. Unlike the others, who had brought food and left, she sat down at the dining table, obviously expecting to eat with us. It was so hard for me to even think about food. I had not eaten a drop since Friday night. Now it was Monday night and we had a houseful of guests, including Paco's parents.

Somehow I managed to get the table set and everyone sat down for a meal. After dinner had been served, Paco's parents and the others dismissed themselves from the table and I stayed on at the table with the flight attendant. She was sharing her physical problems with me. Her ears had been hurting, making it difficult for her to fly. Even on the ground, her ears were ringing and burning. She had been to a few doctors, but none were able to help her. As I listened, I decided to make a bold move. For the first time in my life, I offered to pray for someone out loud.

"Dear Jesus," I prayed. "You know better than we do what is wrong with her ears. You created her, knitting her together in her mother's womb. Please heal her today. Let her ears be made whole. I command these ears to line up with the pure and perfect will and Word of God. Be healed now, in the name of Jesus."

"Thank you so much, Vicki. I really appreciate your prayers. All of this time I've been dealing with this problem, I honestly hadn't thought to ask anyone for prayer." Whether she was healed or not, I never knew. I never saw her again. However, one thing was certain. I had changed. The fear of praying aloud had obviously been broken during my weekend of terror. My self-consciousness had also been altered. Praying for her needs had taken my mind off of my own needs.

"Lord Jesus," I prayed silently, "give me the ability to reach past my own pain to serve the needs of others during this difficult time. Transport me past my own problems and help me to see others needs." That single prayer was to become the foundation for the next few years of my spiritual life. I never forgot the peace I had felt praying for someone else's need on the evening of my own son's funeral. There was a power and a peace in praying for others that transcended my personal pain.

The next morning, Paco's parents were sitting with us around the kitchen table, when the phone rang. We had all been crying, still trying to fathom how our lives could be so changed in such a short period of time. I got up and answered the phone.

"Vicki, I need to speak to Paco. This is Bob."

My mind raced to remember what Bob we knew that knew my name. The person on the other end sounded so impersonal, I could not imagine it would be anyone who knew what our family had just been through. Paco went to the phone. Understandably, in the midst of his grief, it was hard to speak. Clearing his throat, Paco finally managed to get out a greeting.

"Who could that be?" I wondered. I still could not identify the cold tone of voice with which I had just spoken. Paco obviously knew the caller and made some small talk before saying, "Sure, Bob. Sure. I'll get right on it."

When he hung up, he said, "That was Bob, our pastor. He has some things he wanted to add to the church newsletter and wondered how soon I could get started on the changes. He seems to be in a hurry for it, all of a sudden."

The monthly newsletter was not due for a few more weeks. I was furious. How could a man of God who had been our pastor make such a thoughtless, impersonal phone call the day after we just buried our infant son? We both sat stunned, each of us wondering the same thing. How could we ever consider him to be our pastor again? Obviously, we could not. As young Christians, still less than three years old in the Lord, we learned some valuable lessons that weekend. In the absence of love, as it says in I Corinthians 13, Christians are just clanging cymbals. Bob's selfishness was a painful reminder that not all shepherds are true shepherds of the flock. Within six weeks, we had made the decision to start shopping for a church where the love of Christ was visible in the pastor.

Nearly a month after the baby died, we got together again with Jerry and Janie. She looked beautiful in her red suit, as she stepped out of the car to greet us. We were all going together to the Full

Gospel Businessman's meeting that was scheduled that evening in downtown Dallas. Jerry was equally dapper in his business suit. Paco and I climbed into the back seat, as Jerry drove to the event. Although time had lapsed since the baby died, we were still hurting in such a great way. Our hearts ached in our son's absence. As much as we wanted to lead normal lives, there was always the inner knowledge that we were different now. No matter how normal we looked on the outside, we were broken vessels within.

I clutched my fingers into a fist to fight the urge to scratch my stomach. I had developed an intense rash on my abdomen that seemed to be getting worse by the day. I had been to the doctor earlier that week at Paco's insistence. We were still hurting financially. Unable to afford health insurance, we only went to the doctor if it was absolutely necessary. After scratching the rash raw, it had spread from my middle to my hip area. Now my entire midsection seemed to be on fire. The doctor couldn't identify the rash. Giving me some topical cream, he thought it may have been caused from the stress I had been experiencing in my life or from the trauma of labor and delivery. Even after applying the cream faithfully, there was no relief.

We chatted through dinner, anxious to hear the speaker share his testimony. I had never been to one of these meetings, but so far it seemed like such a great way to give a testimony to a captive audience during dinner. When the main speaker got up to share, I was immediately taken by his story. What a man of faith he was. Unable to read or write, he had passed all of his tests for a GED by relying solely on God's answers to the questions in front of him. His parents had named him "Oop" at birth, and as a grown man, he had never changed it. As he was sharing his testimony, in mid-sentence, he stopped. "There it is. The Holy Spirit!" Then he continued to finish his sentence. It happened so quickly those who were not paying attention surely missed it. However, I was listening intently. At the exact moment that he stopped and said, "There it is. The Holy Spirit," I felt a strange warming sensation sweep over my body. It felt as though someone had poured a bucket of hot oil over my head. The feeling started at my head and continued down to my toes. I had never felt anything quite like it. I looked over at Janie on my right then over to Paco on my left to see if either of them had felt the heat. They were both looking straight ahead. Neither of them seemed to have been touched.

I was experiencing such a heavy touch of the Holy Spirit, I practically floated home that night. I had not even thought about my rash and the insatiable itching I had been experiencing for weeks. As I prepared for bed that night, I looked at my skin in amazement. It was as though God had literally replaced my old skin with new skin. All of the raised red welts with bloody lines were replaced with perfect skin.

"Paco," I screamed with delight. "Come look at what God did tonight. Remember me telling you about the awesome touch of heat I received tonight from the Holy Spirit? He healed me!"

I could hardly believe my eyes. I had seen God heal someone else's body, but now he had healed my body. It was more than I could conceive. I sat down cross-legged on my bed and burst into tears.

"What's the matter, honey? Aren't you happy to be healed?'

"It's not that, honey. I'm thrilled to be healed. I just can't imagine how God can love me so much. I didn't even ask God to do that for me. He just did it. I can't even comprehend how much He loves me."

Paco put his arms around me and his eyes locked onto mine. "He does love us more than we can imagine. It's one of those things I don't know if we will ever really understand."

With each passing day, I felt I was able to get a closer glimpse of God and His perfect, holy love. As I studied His word and prayed for His perfect will in our lives, He became more and more of a personal, living part of my everyday life.

A few weeks later, we were at the office when the phone rang for Paco. He and I had combined our offices so that we could make more efficient use of our time and resources. Now that I did not have any employees, it made sense for us to work together, even if we were working in separate businesses. After he hung up, he came over to my private office to fill me in on the conversation.

"Guess who that was?" I could not imagine.

"Who?" I asked. Obviously, whoever it was, Paco was pleased.

"That was one of the pastors from Church on the Rock in Rockwall. They want me to do a billboard for them."

"How did they ever find out about you? We have never gone to church there. Who gave them your name?"

"They said they called the billboard company, who gave them my name and number. They had seen the billboard I did for the rock 'n roll station and thought it was cool. So they want me to do a billboard for them along the same lines. They are looking for something that is modern and different. Something people would not expect to see on a church billboard."

"Do they even know that you are a Christian?" I asked. We had actually headed toward that church several times on different occasions, only to turn back because we did not want to show up late. Now, the Lord was obviously intervening to make sure that we found our way to that church.

"I told them I was a Christian," Paco beamed. His face was flushed with pride from the flattery of the call. Standing a bit taller, he said, "They said they would drop by the office and talk to me about the billboard. When I have some concepts, I can bring them to the church service on Sunday to discuss them after the service."

I just shook my head in awe. I had a premonition that this church was to become more to us than a new account. Even I could not have imagined how accurate a premonition that was. Church on the Rock quite literally changed our lives.

It was the last Sunday of the year. 1982 was almost over. I breathed a deep sigh of relief just thinking about it as we scurried around the house, getting ourselves and our three- and one-year old daughters ready for church.

"What a year this has been," I sighed as we got into the car to head out to Church on the Rock. "Something good has to happen before this year is over. Maybe today will be the day."

As we entered the church, there was a buzz and an excitement that I had never experienced in a church. The praise and worship service was powerful. The preaching was to the point and convicting. I looked over at Paco to see if he felt as strongly about the service as I did. His smile and wink confirmed it.

After the service he met with the staff to discuss their advertising needs and his concepts for the new billboard. As he walked toward the car, there was a bounce to his step I had not seen in awhile. As I climbed into the car, Paco looked over at me and smiled. "They loved the concepts we came up with. They want to do it." I leaned over and gave him a strong hug.

"It looks like we have found our church home."

"I think so," Paco said. "I really think so."

It is hard to describe how Church on the Rock impacted our Christian lives. The people we met there were so sold out to God. There seemed to be an expectancy in the air that we had never witnessed at any other church. Without a doubt, things were happening at Church on the Rock.

We enrolled in the "Finding the Rock" 10-week class for new members. This class was a prerequisite to church membership. It taught all of the basic fundamental teachings of the New Testament church and how believers are to act in a New Testament church.

Although Paco and I felt we had learned a lot about the Bible in our three years as believers, we were anxious to see what the "Finding the Rock" class taught. Once we finished that class, we would start the next 10-week class based on Watchman Nee's book, Spiritual Authority. After that, if we wanted to become small group leaders, there was another 10-week class we would need to attend. I loved the structure of the classes. We always enjoyed working in our workbook together and would discuss the concepts in depth with one another in the privacy of our own home.

Since the death of our son, we had continued to experience the Lord in special ways. I spent hours at night after the girls were in bed, studying the Word and praying that God would show me the reasons He saw fit to allow our son to die a premature death.

One night, as I was reading the book of John, Chapter 17, I had a revelation. As Jesus was praying in the garden of Gethsemane, He said to the Father, "I have finished the work You have given Me to do." I stopped reading and put my Bible down. My sister, Marcia, had given me the Amplified Bible as a gift when Paquito died. I looked up the scripture in the Amplified Bible, "I have glorified You down here on the earth by completing the work that You gave Me to do." I meditated on the scripture.

Jesus was just thirty-three years old when he died a tragic, premature death. In the world's eyes, he died an untimely death.

However, the Bible also says that if Satan had known how Jesus was to be glorified, he never would have crucified the King of Glory.

"Lord," I prayed. "Is it possible that you had a fifty day mission on this earth for our son? Had our son already completed his work here on the earth? Did he bring glory to your name, Lord Jesus, through his life and through his death?"

I felt an all-encompassing peace resting upon my spirit, and I knew I had stumbled onto a truth. In the fifty days our son lived, he had impacted our lives and the lives of our families and friends in a way few people ever do.

"Lord," I prayed. "Show me more of the puzzle. I know you said he was called to be a Nazarite. What exactly does it mean to be a Nazarite? As I started to flip through my concordance to find the Biblical references to a Nazarite, my spirit was encouraged. I found two times in the Bible where the babies born were to be Nazarites. One was the verse of scripture in Judges 13:7 where Sampson's parents were told their son was to be a Nazarite.

The other was John the Baptist. And of course, Jesus was a Nazarite. "What did those three lives have in common, Lord?" I prayed as I continued to study the passages before me. And then I saw it. **They were all born to die untimely deaths that glorified the Lord.** They were sacrificed. I thought about that for a while; like Elizabeth and Mary, my son's life was also cut short supernaturally. Each of them knew their children were going to be special. The Holy Spirit had spoken to each of them concerning their sons before their births. My heart leapt within me. Like those women, I was called from the foundations of the world to give birth to a child that would glorify God the Father in his death. I wondered if Sampson's mother, Elizabeth or Mary had also felt confused and alone when their "special sons" died untimely deaths.

Of course, Mary's grief was soon turned to joy when it was revealed to her that her son had resurrected. Even Mary, though, had been called at a great sacrifice to ride a donkey when she was nine months pregnant to a distant town. And while she was there, she gave birth in a dirty, old barn with animals in it. She had to have wondered, from time to time, if she was truly favored among women. And what of Sampson's mother and Elizabeth? Did they spend the rest of their lives wondering why God had allowed their sons to die early, tragic deaths? I closed my Bible, satisfied at last with the knowledge that my little Nazarite was in God's perfect will, even if it did seem like cruel and unusual punishment at the time. As I slipped into sleep that night, I felt an ember of hope fanning in my spirit. Maybe, just maybe, God was not finished with us yet.

Shortly after that, I opened my Amplified Bible to Isaiah 30:18. "And therefore the Lord [earnestly] waits [expectant, looking and longing] to be gracious to you; and therefore He lifts Himself up, that He may have mercy on you and show loving kindness to you. For the Lord is a God of justice. Blessed (happy, fortunate, to be envied) are all those who [earnestly] wait for Him, who expect and look and long for Him (for His victory, His favor, His love, His peace, His joy, and His matchless, unbroken companionship)!"

"Wow," I thought, as I meditated on that verse. "What a wonderful verse. 'For the Lord is a God of justice....' If God is truly a just God, then who am I to say that the death of my son was unjust?" The thought really took root in me as I meditated on it some more. I thought of the horrific description of John the Baptist's death in the Bible. Here John had been so convinced that Jesus was the Light of the World, he staked his entire reputation on it. He had lived an uncompromising life, unwilling to conform to the world, based on his fervent, passionate conviction that he was to light the way in the wilderness, in preparation of the coming of the Messiah. Yet, as he sat wasting away in prison, he began to doubt. He even sent messengers to ask Jesus if He was truly the One, or if they were to wait for another. How confused he must have been at that moment. I am sure he was thinking something along these lines: "If Jesus of Nazareth is really the Son of God, I would not be sitting here, rotting in jail. I gave my entire life to serve him. Surely, if He were the Savior, He would rescue me from my untimely death. Not only is He the Lamb of the World. We have a special relationship. He is my cousin and my friend. He and I have had some very special, anointed times together. Getting me out of here should be a piece of cake. So why has He just left me here to die? Jesus, where are You?"

I was beginning to understand a little better myself. Just as John was second-guessing God in jail, I had second-guessed God when my son died. Just understanding that God cannot be unjust gave me great comfort. **Although life is not fair, God is.**

If I was to serve God in this "all out capacity," as John had and as Sampson had and especially as Jesus had on earth, I was going to have to settle once and for all the justness of God, no matter what. To this day, the lesson I learned that day has ministered to me when I have heard of other seemingly unjust events in a person's life.

As I spent quality time with the Lord at night, the Lord was rewarding me in my business during the day. Our financial struggles had multiplied over the three months since our son's death. Since both Paco and I were self-employed, we relied on our client's business for income. After our son's death, clients seemed to be avoiding us and we were going into deep debt. The bills were piling up so quickly, I was not even opening them anymore. Our water was even turned off for non-payment.

In discussing it with Paco, I tried to pinpoint what was bothering me. "It is as though everyone near us had some sort of morbid curiosity when our son died. People poured out of the woodwork in the days that followed his death. Yet, a few months later, it seems as though no one will have anything to do with us. It's almost as if they don't know what to say or how to act around us. If they would just call and ask how we are doing, or stop by to say they love us and they are praying for us, it would help. It just seems as though everyone we know has scattered."

Paco agreed. "I do think the whole episode makes people feel uncomfortable, so they would just as well go elsewhere. Or maybe our clients feel like they should not bother us in the wake of our traumatic event. Whatever. This lack of business is killing us for sure."

Just when it looked as though we were going to lose our business, our home, our cars and anything else we owned, the Lord pulled through. I made a sale just before the end of the year that delivered us from our debt overnight. As I called my sister, Marcia, and gave her my praise report, she was in awe of God's faithfulness toward us. "What a miracle, Vic. To think that in one transaction, God could reverse your situation. That is amazing." It was an unusual financial miracle. In a single moment, we went from the brink of financial disaster to having enough money in the bank to pay our bills for several months. The sale happened just before the end of 1982. It had been a roller coaster year we would never forget.

"So the men came to Jesus and said, John the Baptist sent us to You to ask, are You the One Who is to come, or shall we continue to look for another? In that very hour, Jesus was healing many [people] of sicknesses and distressing bodily plagues and evil spirits, and to many who were blind He gave [a free, gracious, joy-giving gift of] sight.

He replied to them, Go tell John what you have seen and heard: the blind receive their sight, the lame walk, the lepers are cleansed, the deaf hear, the dead are raised up, and the poor have the good news (the Gospel) preached to them. And blessed (happy - with life-joy and satisfaction in God's favor and salvation, apart from outward conditions - and to be envied) is he who takes no offense in Me and who is not hurt or resentful or annoyed or repelled or made to stumble [whatever may occur]."

Luke 7:20-23

"The Lord will perfect that which concerns me, Your mercy and loving-kindness, Oh Lord, endure forever - forsake not the works of Your own hands."

Psalm 138:8

"I will cry to God Most High, who performs on my behalf and rewards me [who brings to pass His purposes for me and surely completes them]!"

Psalm 57:2

CHAPTER 5

The Season Of Healing Miracles

≫

For as horrible a year as 1982 was, the following year proved to be a special blessing from the Lord. Although my arms ached to hold my baby boy, the Lord truly did give me a special grace to walk through the aftermath of his death. I had determined to reach out to minister to someone else each time I felt the dreaded shadow of grief looming over my soul. Through the months that followed my son's death, praying for others was the only antidote I had found that really worked. Each time I prayed for someone else and truly entered into his or her pain, I experienced a fresh touch of God's grace to walk out my own grief.

In early April, I was home one morning when I clearly heard the Lord speak to me. "When the phone call comes, go."

Although I could not imagine to what the Lord was referring, I guarded the word in my heart. I did not have to wait long. Just after lunch, the phone rang. It was my Mom. My Grandmother had been diagnosed with colon cancer.

"Nothing to be concerned about," Mom said. "It is just a routine operation. She will be home in no time."

"Mom," I said, "I have to come up. I will make reservations today and be there before she has her operation on Monday."

"That really will not be necessary, Vic. The doctors have

assured us it is not life threatening. Just a routine procedure."

"I understand what you are saying, Mom, but I really do have to come. Can you pick me up Sunday?"

"Of course we can. Just let us know what time you are flying in and we will be there."

As I hung up the phone, I stood at my kitchen counter staring blankly out the window. The word I had heard from the Lord just hours earlier echoed through my mind. "When the phone call comes, go." Obviously, the Lord knew something my parents and the doctors did not. As it turned out, if I had not gone to be with my Grandmother before her surgery, I never would have seen her alive again.

When I walked into the hospital room, Grandma Ann was her usual jolly self. She was always very joyful around me, acting as though I had just brought the sunshine in with me. Actually, she was known to most as a very cantankerous woman. But with me, she had never been anything but loving and kind. We shared a very special relationship.

"Oh Ann, I love you so much," I thought. "You can't even imagine what your love has meant to me." It struck me, as I sat beside her bed, holding her hand and making small talk, that I actually knew very little about her. For the first time, I tried to imagine her as a young woman, preparing for her wedding day. As I sat there by her bed, studying the soft folds of her chin and her laughing, milk chocolate-colored eyes, I wondered if she had any idea how much she had impacted my life. Although she was not my blood relative, she was the only Grandmother I had ever really known.

I tried to imagine her first meeting with my own mother, when my Mom was just a young teen, and the conversation that ensued. Ann and her husband, Lyman, had asked my Mother if she would like to come live with them. A childless couple, with a lot of love to give, they gave sanctuary to my Mom at a very tender time in her life, when her single dad did not know how he was going to raise her alone. And so my Mom had moved into the Bush home, to be raised through her teen years by Ann and Lyman, in a very small, rural town in Upstate New York, just thirty miles from her own home. Before long, she fell in love with the boy across the street, my Dad. After marrying, it was only natural that my parents would stay on in North Cohocton, living just a few houses up from my Dad's childhood home and the Bush home.

My earliest memories all included Ann. Ann teaching me to bake cinnamon rolls, chiding me gently as I imitated the way she had shown me to knead the dough. Ann watching me sew as I practiced with a needle and thread, a careful eye correcting my awkward, uneven stitches. I thought of the many times she had sat on her front porch and waited for a glimpse of me, so she could open her screen door and yell out, "Vicki Miller, you get yourself in here right now." It never failed. I knew the minute I passed in front of her house, I was obliged to pop in to the front porch and give her a big hug and kiss and a quick update on my day.

Ann definitely played a leading roll in my life. She was my anchor and my safe harbor. We were soul mates and best friends. My eyes filled with tears as I remembered the tender moments we had spent together – a lifetime of moments, really.

I recalled with vivid detail that fateful day in late November 1960, when Lyman was killed in a tragic car accident. Ann sat on a hard chair in our living room, her purse perched on her lap, weeping uncontrollably into her white hankie. Deep, wrenching sobs filled our home, as we all just sat lifeless, numbed by the horrible news. I was just four, yet as I sat beside her in the hospital room that day in 1983, the scene replayed afresh in my mind. The pain was so great that day, and yet I could not cry. I could only sit and watch Ann and wish that it could all be different for her. With all my heart, I wanted to reach out to her, to heal her broken heart. But the chair she was sitting on was way too small and hard for two people to snuggle. No. The time just did not seem right. I decided I would wait and let some time pass. Soon enough, I would be alone with Ann in her small kitchen and I would sit on her lap and let her rock me. That would be soothing to her and to me. Just as I imagined it, in late January, on Ann's 58th birthday, she scooped me up in her arms and we cried together as she rocked me by her kitchen table. It was a deep, moving experience I had never forgotten. Though few words were spoken that day, we communicated with one another in a language we both understood.

"Ann needs me so much now that Lyman's gone," I thought. I

vowed to stop in more often to see her. And until she signaled otherwise, I decided I would always crawl quickly into her lap and let her rock me. Even when I was a senior in high school, Ann would sometimes rock me. Yes, indeed. Ann was one of those very special women that every little girl needs in her life to make it through. I would miss her greatly. I tried to bring my mind back to happier thoughts.

"Annie-fanny!" I joked with her. "Did you bring any curlers so I could set your hair for you?"

"Of course I did. I brought my pin curls."

I could not believe she still had her pin curls. I had not seen them in ages. I sat playing with the soft, oddly shaped pink curlers that seemed to magically snap into place on her head after her hair was rolled. "Boy, does this bring back a lot of memories," I thought.

"Well, sit down here in the chair and I'll curl your hair for you."

We joked and laughed with each other while I curled her hair, just like I did every Saturday night for years. It was just like old times.

Before the nurse came to take her to surgery, I drew close to her and took her hand. "Ann," I said seriously. "I have something I need to talk to you about – something that's very important to me."

"Oh, I meant to tell you how sorry I was to hear about your baby," Ann interjected. "That was a terrible thing."

"It was a terrible thing, Ann. I would not wish it on anyone. But it was so much easier to go through because I have the Lord in my life now. I don't think I ever really told you about how I asked Jesus to come into my heart."

Ann listened intently as I recounted to her how I had run down the aisle of that Baptist church just four years earlier and committed my life to Christ. Somehow, I knew, because she cared so much about me, it would mean something to her to know that I had such a special relationship with Jesus. When I had finished, I drew my face even closer to hers.

"Ann, I need to ask you something: Have you ever given your heart to Jesus?" Her answer surprised me.

"Yes, I did," she responded, matter-of-factly. "When I was eighteen years old, I asked Jesus to come into my heart."

"That is wonderful, Ann. Would you like to recommit your life to Him right now, so you can go into your surgery knowing that you are at peace with the Lord?"

She nodded her head, and then bowed to pray. I was so choked with emotion, I had a difficult time leading her in the sinner's prayer:

"Lord Jesus, thank You for dying on the cross for me. Right now, I repent of my sins and trust Your shed blood as full payment for all my sins. I believe that You are the Son of God and that God has raised You from the dead. I now receive You as my personal Savior and commit my life unreservedly to You as Lord. Thank You for hearing my prayer; forgiving my sins, and coming into my life as You promised. Amen."

When we finished, I took her pin curls out and brushed her hair for her. Before long, the nurse popped her head into the room.

"Ann, we need to take you to pre-op now. Your granddaughter can follow us down, and then I am afraid she will have to leave."

"I would like to pray over the surgeon's hands, if I could. Is he available for prayer?" I asked boldly. The nurse seemed taken aback, then a slight smile crossed her face.

"I don't think he will mind. Let me see if I can find him for you."

A short time later, I was driving home, thinking about the morning I had with Ann and the prayer I prayed over the surgeon, hoping God would honor it. I felt warm and happy, as I recollected my parting conversation with Ann. It was quick, yet sweet and not too hurried. The nurse allowed me to take the time I needed to kiss and hug her one last time, combing my hands through her hair with my fingers.

"I love you, Ann. I always will."

"I love you, too, Vicki."

Our eyes locked one last time. Then she was wheeled away. I stood and watched as her stretcher moved methodically down the long corridor, then disappeared from sight. In my spirit, I knew the next time I saw her would be in heaven. A few days later, Ann died from complications from her surgery.

April of 1983 proved to be a turning point in my life. The day after I got home from my trip to New York, I received a distress call from a friend of mine from Church on the Rock. She was keeping her grandchildren and was extremely concerned about her five-year old grandson, Jonathan, who had been experiencing recurring nightmares that were so deep and disturbing, it sometimes took twenty minutes for her to wake him out of them. She had just been through a bout the night before and wondered if I would pray with him. I was very honest with Billie about my lack of experience in prayer, and recommended that she contact one of the pastors from the church. I was exhausted from my trip and did not feel spiritually prepared to offer up prayer for anyone.

"Please, Vicki," she persisted. "I really don't feel comfortable taking Jonathan anywhere else. I need someone who will be sensitive to him. I just know Jonathan will feel comfortable with you."

I gave in under her insistence.

"Okay, I will see you in a few minutes."

I quickly changed out of my robe and ran around the house, picking it up as fast as I could. The house was a total mess. I vividly remember how tired and lethargic I felt that morning, and how overwhelmed I was at the idea of anyone visiting on such late notice. I really did not feel up to having company. I especially did not feel strong enough to have someone drop by for an intense prayer session.

"Oh Lord, please bless our time together this morning," I prayed under my breath, as I ran to answer the door.

Billie came in with her two grandchildren and I ushered her to the kitchen table as the children ran into my kid's bedrooms to play. We sat at the table for a few minutes, as I shared with Billie how I felt Jonathan would feel most comfortable. "I thought I would sit all of the kids in here on the floor together and say a short prayer over each of them, then send each one off to play in the bedroom. I will save Jonathan for last, so he doesn't feel singled out." Billie agreed. The kids were wonderful. Not quite yet two and four, I was most concerned about whether my two would comply. Fortunately, they all went along with the plan. When I got to Jonathan, all of the other children had already left the room.

"Come here, sweetie. Before I pray for you, I want to talk to you for a minute. Your grandma says you are having really bad dreams. Do you remember them?" He shrugged his shoulders.

"Not usually. Sometimes I do."

I glanced at Billie, trying to figure out if I needed to probe him further. I decided against it, and started to pray. After the prayer, I looked back at Billie to see if she was satisfied. She seemed to be. She nodded, and then added, "Do you mind praying for his eyes? Jonathan has had so many problems in his young life with his eyes. He has had several eye surgeries the past few years and has been diagnosed as being legally blind."

"That is terrible, Billie. I had no idea." I scooted around on the floor, cross-legged, and looked intensely into Jonathan's eyes. They were huge behind the "coke-bottle" lenses. He was wearing a patch over one of his eyes.

"Just to give you an idea of how bad his vision really is, he walked into a parked car a few nights ago," Billie added.

"Are you serious? That's unbelievable." I could not imagine how bad Jonathan's eyes really were. I just sat there for a minute, trying to comprehend how his poor eyesight must affect everything in his young life.

"Jonathan, honey," I said, matter-of-factly. "Do you believe that Jesus can heal your eyes?"

"Yes, I do," he said with conviction. "But I have to warn you, I have had the best pray for me."

His statement took me by surprise. "What do you mean, when you say 'the best' have prayed for you?"

"You know what I mean," he responded, sounding slightly exasperated. "The best pastors. Pastor Larry Lea, Oral Roberts. You know."

"Oral Roberts prayed for your eyes to be healed?" I asked incredulously.

"Yeah, he did," he exclaimed. Then his voice dropped low and he stared at the floor for a minute, before adding, "but they weren't." A wave of pity swept over me. I could not fathom being five years old and suffering the disappointment of unanswered prayer. I felt a renewed sense of indignation at the entire situation.

"Do you believe Jesus can heal your eyes today?"

He did not hesitate in his answer.

"Yes, I do."

"Well, alright then, let's pray right now and ask Jesus to give you 20/20 vision. Do you have faith to believe He can give you perfect eyesight?" He gave his head an emphatic affirmative nod. I looked back over at Billie. "What exactly do the doctors say Jonathan has? Is it a disease?"

"Myopia and strabismus," Billie said.

"They sound demonic to me. I am going to take authority over those diseases in the name of Jesus."

I took Jonathan's glasses off of him and removed his eye patch. Then I asked him to lie down on the floor. I grabbed for my anointing oil and touched his forehead with it, reminding the Lord of the scripture in James 5:15 where Christians are instructed to anoint the sick with oil and pray for them and they will be healed. "In the name of Jesus Christ of Nazareth, I bind all demonic activity over Jonathan today. I bind you, Satan, and every principality, power, spirit and assignment ruling and operating over Jonathan's life today. I bind the rulers of this world and the princes of darkness over Jonathan's life. I command you, myopia and strabismus, to leave Jonathan in the name of Jesus. You cannot rule and operate over his eyes, in the name of Jesus Christ. Come out of him, now!"

"Jonathan, honey. Look at me." He opened his eyes and looked at me. I put up two fingers in front of his face. "How many fingers do I have up?"

He blinked a few times and then shook his head.

"I can't see your fingers. They are just shadows," he said dejectedly.

I stopped and thought about it for a minute. All of the scriptures I had learned after the baby died came running through my head.

"In Matthew 18, the Word says Jesus has given us the keys to the kingdom and whatsoever we bind on heaven is bound on earth. That includes myopia and strabismus. In the name of Jesus Christ of Nazareth, I command every demonic spirit ruling and operating over Jonathan's life to leave immediately. By the power vested in me as a child of the Living King, you have to leave now. You cannot stay in the name of Jesus. You must bow to the name of Jesus."

Although I was speaking with authority, I never raised my voice above a hushed whisper.

"Now, Jonathan, sweetie. Open your eyes and tell me how many fingers I have raised."

The look on his face was priceless, as he yelled out, "Two! I see two fingers!"

I changed to four then to three then to five. Each time, he answered quickly and emphatically, unable to contain his excitement. "I can see, Grandma. I can see!"

Billie and I were elated.

"Would you mind coming to the house with me to pray over the house?" Billie asked. "I don't think his parents would mind if you anointed the house in their absence."

I was definitely feeling a huge burst of confidence. My exhaustion had taken a back seat to the waves of adrenalin that were now flowing through my veins. I had never personally prayed and received such an awesome answer to prayer. My head was spinning with excitement.

"I would love to go to your house. I will drive behind you. Let's go to lunch at McDonalds first."

Billie quickly agreed, so we gathered the kids up and headed for McDonalds.

"I want to ride in the Garza's car," Jonathan yelled, as he climbed into the backseat. It was so great to see his enthusiasm. I was thrilled to have him with us. As we drove down the highway, the golden arches of McDonalds peeked into view beyond the hill. "I see the golden arches," Jonathan squealed with glee.

"He really can see," I thought. I still could not really fathom how a simple prayer offered in faith by a tired, young mom could stir the heart of God to heal a little boy's eyes. "Jonathan's faith was great," I thought. "And both Billie and I believed God could do it."

Yet, now that He had healed Jonathan, I was incredulous.

The rest of the day raced by. I anointed their home and had come back to the house when I realized I had left my purse there. When I called Billie to see if I could come by to pick it up, she asked me to come around dinnertime.

As I walked through the front door, I could not believe my eyes.

Jonathan was sitting at the dinner table with his pirate patch and coke-bottle glasses on.

I felt righteous indignation rising up within me.

"Billie," I was trying to conceal my irritation. "What are you doing? Jonathan can see. He does not need those things on his eyes now." Billie looked down and away, like a child who had been caught. Then she gathered her courage and addressed me.

"Vicki, you don't have any idea how much this family has been through with Jonathan's eyes. He's had years of treatment and eye exercises. And he is only five. I just don't feel I have the authority to remove his patch and his glasses. When his parents come home, I will let them make that decision. I just really do not want to reverse years of treatment. Do you see where I am coming from?"

I did understand what she was saying and yet, I knew his parents well. I was fairly certain they would be very quick to receive Jonathan's healing in a positive light. I thought for a minute. Then, I had an idea.

"Billie, if I call an ophthalmologist and set up an appointment to have Jonathan's eyes tested, will you accept his test results as reason enough to remove the patch and the glasses?"

"Fair enough," Billie agreed. "If his eyes test out positively, I will take the patch and the glasses off."

The next morning I arranged to have Jonathan's eyes tested. Billie and I took Jonathan to the ophthalmologist together, without his coke-bottle glasses and pirate patch. "Please Jesus," I prayed. "Please let his eyes be perfect."

The ophthalmologist seemed a little puzzled as to why we were in his office.

"Why did you bring Jonathan in this morning?" he asked.

"We are here to have Jonathan's eyes tested. We just want to make sure everything is alright with his eyes."

He eyed us suspiciously. I wondered what he was thinking. For a minute, I thought he was going to refuse to test him. Then he slowly reached for his screening machine and began to ask Jonathan which lens was better: "This one? Or this one? This one? Or this one? This one? Or this one?"

Billie and I sat in the corner, wringing our hands nervously. I was trying to breathe deep and remain calm. Finally he was finished with the machine and he referred Jonathan to the eye chart. "Which of these lines can you read?"

"All of them," Jonathan exclaimed. "I can read all of the letters." Billie and I sat and listened as Jonathan read off the letters perfectly.

"I knew it," I thought excitedly. "He does have perfect vision."

I turned to the doctor. "Well? Is his vision 20/20?"

Again, he hesitated. I could tell he was still wondering why we were there. "He does have perfect vision. Is there anything else you needed to know?"

Billie moved forward on her seat, speaking for the first time. "I have a question, doctor. Do you see any scar tissue in his eyes?"

The doctor seemed perplexed. I could tell the question bothered him. He answered Billie in a very deliberate way.

"I did not study his eyes for scar tissue specifically. Would you like me to do that at this time?"

"Oh, yes. That is, if you do not mind, doctor. That would be great."

The doctor took his time with his instrument, studying Jonathan's eyes intently. Finally, he turned back to us.

"I do not see any evidence of any type of scar tissue. His eyes are perfect."

Billie and I looked at each other in amazement. We were both about ready to burst from the elation. "Thank you so much, doctor. We really appreciate the extra time you took with us this morning," we cooed as we ran out of the room with Jonathan. Once in the parking lot, we all jumped up and down with joy.

"Billie," I said emphatically. "Under no circumstances do I want to see a patch or glasses on Jonathan's eyes again. Do you promise me you will put them away forever?"

"I promise," she beamed. "Can you believe this, Vicki? God is so good."

"Amen," I agreed. "Amen."

The next morning in church, Pastor Larry gave the praise report to the congregation. Without mentioning my name, he said, "A young mother from the church prayed for one of the boys in our congregation that was legally blind and Jesus healed his eyes. An ophthalmologist tested him yesterday and confirmed that he has 20/20 vision."

Then he gave an invitation to the congregation and asked anyone who believed the Lord could heal their eyes to come forward for corporate prayer. Quite a few people went to the altar that day for prayer. Later, one of the pastors on staff told me that five people had confirmed cases of healing in their eyes that Sunday.

"Lord, you are such an awesome God," I thought. I was reminded of David's writing in Psalm 8:4, "What is man that you are mindful of him?"

My mind wandered back to just over six months earlier, when our young son died in his sleep. And the day we buried him, when I dared to pray out loud for the first time.

"I am still such an infant in the Lord," I mused. "God, You know, I honestly do not understand any of this. Please reveal to me how prayer works."

My life literally took on a new dimension of faith from that day forward. I knew that I knew, with God, all things were absolutely possible. I threw myself into the study of the Word, the memorization of scripture and intense times of intercessory prayer. It was an exciting and thrilling time in my life, laced with intense grieving over the recent death of my son.

Although I never grieved openly, I often cried late at night, when I knew Paco and the children were asleep. When I could not sleep, my thoughts would turn to my empty arms and aching heart. I would imagine him in heaven and wonder what it was like for him there. And wonder, if he had lived, what he would look like. I wondered if he knew how much we missed him. And if he missed us. Often, it seemed as though I could still smell his soft, baby scent in our bedroom, as if he was still in his bassinet beside our bed.

I knew God knew my pain. And I knew He had sent me this beautiful time of answered prayer as a special gift to get me through. Every time I prayed with others for their needs, my faith soared and my spirits lifted.

One night, a few months later, Paco and I had gone to one of the weeknight services at church and were standing near the front, when an amazing thing happened. Pastor Larry had asked everyone to take hands across the rows. As everyone was taking hands, he said, "There is someone here tonight who feels as though they are all alone. As you are standing here, you are thinking, 'I do not have a friend in the world.'"

At that moment, the Holy Spirit spoke to my heart and said, "Notice the girl on the end, who does not have anyone to take her hand. I want you to move up to the front row and take her hand." I was suddenly feeling very self-conscious and could feel my face flushing with embarrassment just thinking about it.

"I cannot do that, Lord."

"Yes, you can. Just move up to the front row and take her hand."

My frustration and fear were mounting. I could feel myself holding my breath. I felt as though I would burst. "No, Lord. I cannot do it," I insisted, as I stubbornly refused to move.

"Vicki," the Holy Spirit spoke sternly, "you can. Just do it."

"Alright, Lord. I will."

I took a deep breath and moved forward. As I took my place beside the girl, I pressed my hand firmly into hers. She seemed startled as she glanced over at me. I smiled at her warmly, feeling a fresh anointing of the love of Jesus surge through me. I bowed my head since Pastor Larry was still praying.

"Jesus loves you and He shows it in such wonderful ways. If you will come forward tonight, and give your heart to Him, He will never leave you nor forsake you. Just come forward now and give your life to Him. He will be your best friend."

The girl I was standing with loosed her hand from mine and ran forward, breaking into deep sobs at the altar. She was the only one to go forward to accept the Lord that night. As the pastors moved forward to pray with her, my hands instantly flew into the air in gratitude as I praised Jesus for His goodness. I stood in utter amazement and awe as I struggled to understand what had just happened.

"Oh, Lord Jesus," I prayed. "Please forgive my disobedience. I cannot believe the simple action of taking someone's hand has made an eternal difference in a life. I promise to be more obedient and move out faster when I know you have spoken to me. I believe you know what is best, even when it makes absolutely no sense to my mortal mind. Please help my unbelief."

I never forgot that night and the reverential fear of God I felt as I considered what might have happened had I not obeyed His voice. It was a foundational experience for me. It definitively shaped the form of things to come in my spiritual life.

August 6, 1983, was a hard day for me. My sweet little son would have been one year old. We should have been celebrating his first birthday. Instead, I felt a profound loneliness. Our two girls were spending the week with Paco's family in Mexico, so I did not even have my little ones to pick up and hold.

More than anything, I was feeling forsaken and betrayed by the Lord. I could not seem to pull myself out of the deep pit I found myself in. To top it all off, Paco had a difficult deadline to meet and spent the entire day working from home. All day, I wandered from my room to the kitchen to the dinner table where he was busy drawing. The discontentment was mounting and by dinnertime, I was so miserable I wanted to die.

"Honey, I have to do something. I cannot remain in this state of mind. I feel like I am going crazy. I just feel like no matter how much I pray, I cannot seem to lift myself out of this horrible mood. Can't we do something tonight? It is maddening to feel so alone and have no one to talk to."

"I have to get this job done tonight, honey, or I will never meet my deadline. Why don't you go to the prophetic meeting Helene told you about?" I really did not want to go to the meeting alone. Yet I knew that he couldn't come with me. I decided to go without him. I knew I had to get out of the house and do something.

"Well, okay then, I guess I will go. You don't mind?"

"Of course not, honey. Go ahead and go."

I sat in the meeting wishing I could leave. With every prophetic word that was given to someone else, I was feeling more and more alone. I purveyed the room, studying each face. I did not know anyone there. A few faces looked vaguely familiar, but I did not know anyone personally. I wondered what any one of them was going through that compared to the weight I felt in my heart. I studied the prophetess as she searched the room for the next beneficiary of God's spoken word.

"Me, Lord! Choose me," I screamed silently.

I felt like a schoolgirl waiting to be picked for a softball team. I honestly cannot remember ever feeling more overlooked than I did that night. When the meeting ended, I felt as though I was the only person present that was not ministered to directly. Eventually, everyone started to get up and leave. Soon, other than the hostess, I was the only one left. Slowly, painfully, I got up to leave. I could not believe God would not give me a word of encouragement. I felt like I was down and I had just gotten a swift kick in the teeth.

"Lord, I thought You loved me. Is it too much to ask to get a word from You tonight, on my son's first birthday? Did I drive all the way here to return home empty handed and more dejected than when I came? I can't believe this."

As I neared the door, I tried to pull myself together and be cordial with the prophetess, who was standing in the doorway, waiting to say goodbye to me.

"Did you get what you came for tonight?" she asked with a confident smile.

I could not believe my ears. I wanted to scream, "Am I invisible? Don't you even know that you did not minister to my needs tonight? How insensitive to God's Holy Spirit are you, anyway? Can't you see that I am dying?"

As much as I tried to just nod and leave, I could not. I stopped and looking directly in her eyes, I said, "No, I did not. I came here tonight because I was hurting. If my son had lived, he would have been one year old today. Next to the day of his death and burial, it has been one of the worst days of my life. I expected to get a word from God tonight."

Instantly, I wished I could retract my words. I had obviously caught her off guard and dumped my disappointment on her without any advanced notice. She looked intently into my eyes and did not speak for a moment. When she did, she was genuinely apologetic.

"I am so sorry. Let's ask the Lord for a word for you. Please let me pray for you."

I closed my eyes and hot tears instantly streamed down my cheeks. "Please, Lord, touch me," I prayed silently. "I cannot stand another minute of this darkness in my soul."

She began to speak in tongues as her searing hand pulsated

rhythmically over my forehead. After a few minutes of praying in the spirit, she spoke with an authority in her voice I had not heard all evening. The anointing I felt flowing from her hand onto my forehead was unmistakably the anointing of the Holy Spirit.

"Thus saith the Lord thy God...." Her hand moved to my protruding belly. I was eight months pregnant. "You shall have a son and his name shall be David."

I could not believe my ears. Only God could know that we had called this child David Josiah since we had known we had conceived. We had not told a soul.

"As a young child, he will be like young David...." The prophesy was to the point and beautiful. I wrote it down to give to my son when he was old enough to understand the special blessing and anointing God had for his life. Repeatedly, she mentioned the name David. I was astounded at God's faithfulness. I should have known He would prove Himself to be faithful to me. When I returned to the house that night, I felt as though I had floated home. I had received an unforgettable touch from the Lord at a time when I needed it desperately.

Just a month later, David Josiah made his entrance into the world. Born at home with a midwife, my labor, from start to finish, was just under 45 minutes. Of my six children, he was the only baby that slept all night from the night he was born. He was, indeed, a blessed baby. Holding a baby boy in my arms once again, my empty arms were filled and my broken heart was mended. His life brought a heightened sense of joy and peace to our household that we sorely needed. Finally, there was a settling in our lives that had been missing since the day the baby died. I had a very good feeling that everything was going to be all right now.

> *"...I am convinced and sure of this very thing, that He who began a good work in you will continue until the day of Jesus Christ [right up to the time of His return], developing [that good work] and perfecting and bringing it to full completion in you."*
> *Philippians 1:6*

CHAPTER 6

Called To Africa

∽

In mid-October, when David was just six weeks old, I returned to work. I had been raising funds for a gold mining venture in California with great success earlier in the year. Yet, as I developed my relationship with the principals of the venture, I was feeling increasingly uneasy about the legitimacy of the operation.

I sat down to talk to Paco about my concerns. We decided to freeze the funds until we researched the operation further. I confided my concern to my investors and let them know I was going to be searching for a top-notch geologist that I could hire for an outside opinion on the property.

We found an impressive geologist with an illustrious career in Dallas. The man had an impeccable reputation and a very impressive past. Although he was in his early eighties, he was as sharp as a tack, as they say in Texas. Not only was he mentally sharp, he was one of the most physically robust men I had ever met. Paco and I both felt fortunate to have found such a qualified candidate for our geological consultant. Just a few weeks later, he and Paco flew together to the mining site we were representing to our investors.

On the way home, they flew to another site that our geologist had an interest in exploring. He felt the reports on the property were a bit more impressive than the first site they visited. Paco was not impressed with either site. "I think we will wait and see if we can't find something with more potential than these two mines," Paco told our geologist. "If you don't mind, why don't you let us know whenever you see an opportunity that looks promising. Remember, we are looking for something that has great potential."

Within weeks, the geologist called us. He was very animated as he related to us how he had just returned from a trip to Liberia, West Africa, where there were gold mining claims that were rich with gold. He strongly suggested that he and Paco return to the site on an exploratory mission. They would then return to the states with the samples of gold that could then be assayed at a reputable mining lab in Colorado.

With that one phone call, our lives turned upside down. My first response was to dismiss the suggestion as ludicrous. Both Paco and I saw the entire idea as far-fetched and unrealistic. When we were searching for a mining operation, the thought of an international operation never even crossed our minds. However, deep in my spirit, I felt a witness from the Holy Spirit. After we had some time to let the thought settle, Paco spoke up: "Well? What do you think, honey? I always wanted to go to Africa. How are you feeling about the idea?"

"Well," I said. "I instantly thought he must be insane, but for some odd reason, I feel a witness on it in my spirit. Let's both pray and ask God what He would have us do. If He wants us to go to Africa to invest our investor's money, we will go. If not, we won't. What do you think?"

"Sounds like a plan," Paco said. "I sure wouldn't want to go to Africa if God didn't go with me."

I laughed and agreed. With very little time to deliberate, we set about to pray. After a few days, we both felt, beyond a shadow of a doubt, God was calling us to a gold mining operation in Africa. Once again, our lives had taken a very odd turn.

The last week of November, Paco accompanied our geologist to the site where we would be setting up a working mine. He took enough money with him to get the exploratory operation going. He would be meeting his Liberian partner, an astute banking manager, and they would be visiting the mining claims from there.

Although Paco and our geologist were flying into the capitol city of Monrovia, the claims were many hours from there, deep in the African rain forest. They would be crossing rough terrain in unreliable old jeeps until they came to the last village on the outskirts of the jungle. After that, they would be traveling through the jungle on foot.

I felt perfect peace as Paco prepared for his short trip. Paco was like a little boy under a Christmas tree. Although he had his own business as a graphic designer, his heart was definitely fully engrossed in the plans for the mining operation. At the age of 29, it was a dream come true for him.

His trip came and went. The samples tested out far above what any of us had hoped. I kept calculating and re-calculating, using increasingly lower numbers.

"Honey, even if the price of gold dropped to $200 an ounce, our investors would make their money back many times over! These numbers are incredible." Paco just shook his head in amazement.

"I know it. I just keep thinking I cannot believe this is happening to us, Vic. This is such an awesome opportunity. If God owns the cattle on a thousand hills, surely He knows where the precious metals are, too."

I just looked at Paco and beamed. "He has really come a long way since he first believed," I thought. "We both have."

January 1984 found us busily preparing for our mining operation in Liberia, West Africa. We did not have much time to get malaria medicine and visas for Paco and the two men he had chosen to accompany him. They were childhood friends from Mexico that Paco trusted to stay by his side in a foreign country. They were both accomplished in operating various kinds of heavy equipment, so Paco felt comfortable with the expertise they each lent to the operation.

Paco and the geologist flew to Denver to purchase gold mining machines. When they returned, he and I took a road trip to Houston to buy three trucks, CB radio equipment, mercury (to amalgamate the gold) and a lot of camping equipment. We had everything shipped to the docks in Houston, where we had secured a large container to ship everything to the port in Monrovia, Liberia.

Back at our offices in Dallas, I sat down and made a complete list of everything we had purchased for the trip that was to be included on the Bill of Lading. Our geologist had strongly suggested that both our Liberian partner and Paco's name be included on the Bill of Lading to minimize problems once Paco and his two employees landed in Liberia. As it turned out, that single decision proved to be a very costly one.

From the time Paco and his two men landed in Liberia, there was a problem getting the items off of the dock. Although the container had docked, neither Paco nor his Liberian partner could agree on when to claim the shipment. Our partner wanted to release the goods immediately. Paco demanded to see the gold his Liberian partner had promised was mined by hand by a group of African miners since his trip in November, before they claimed the shipment. Paco had left money with specific restrictions as to how it was to be used when he had last seen his Liberian partner. Now that Paco had returned a few months later, it seemed our partner was stalling and refusing to comply with Paco's requests.

Until the situation was cleared up and the Liberian partner made good on his promises, Paco was hesitant to release anything from the Liberian docks. He knew if he could not trust his partner with the little things, he was not going to be able to trust him for the big things. His hunch was right. Our Liberian partner, as it turned out, was nothing short of a crook.

The first few days of his trip, Paco spent his time getting situated, setting up their housing for the next few months, purchasing groceries and getting a feel for the place. They rented a house on the beach in a compound where American missionaries lived. It was to be their headquarters, where they would head up the mining operation, once it got underway.

As Paco was preparing to visit his partner's offices one more time to see if he would comply with the original demands he had made on the release of the money, he stopped to buy a paper and to get his shoes shined. While his shoes were being shined, he glanced down at the newspaper. There on the front page was a story about his Liberian partner. His partner, it seemed, was under investigation for the disappearance of $40,000 from the bank he managed. He was being charged with embezzlement of the money.

Paper in hand, Paco charged into his partner's office. "What is this?" Paco demanded, angrily slamming the paper down on the desk. "You took your bank's money and now you are taking my investor's money also? I don't think so! You are nothing but a crook. I am going to find myself another Liberian partner – one that I can trust!"

His partner just sat smugly, knowing that his name was on the Bill of Lading and that Paco could not get the shipment off of the docks without him. "Go ahead and find yourself another partner, Mr. Garza. The Bill of Lading is in my name. You won't get far without me," he bellowed.

His eyes narrowed as he sneered at Paco with contempt. Paco glared back in return. Then he stormed out of his office and walked outside to where his friends were waiting. It was a Friday afternoon. The following Monday, Paco went to his landlord's place of business to pay his rent. When he walked outside, a group of Liberian soldiers drove up in two old Army jeeps. "Mr. Garza?" Paco turned, startled to see that a Liberian soldier would know his name. "Get in the vehicle. You and your two friends are being placed under arrest for the possession of dangerous chemicals and illegal communications equipment. We have been informed that you are working in connection with Muammar Qadafi. If these charges prove to be true, you will be sent before the firing squad without a trial. President Samuel Doe does not look kindly on traitors!"

Indignant and enraged, Paco tried vigorously to defend himself to no avail. Finally, realizing they had no choice, he and his friends climbed sheepishly into the back of the truck at gunpoint. They had heard about an execution on the beach just the day before. The four men who were executed had been charged with similar crimes. Paco knew, if the charges could be proven, they could be next.

"Oh Jesus," Paco prayed fervently. "If ever I needed you, I need you now!"

Paco and his friends were taken to the local authorities for interrogation. Miraculously, the sergeant in charge agreed to allow the three men to be placed under tight surveillance, rather than locking them up in the local jail. Due to the terrible economic conditions in Liberia, the people were impoverished. Although the government was operating under military law, even the military had not been paid in months. In response to continual harassment by drunken

Liberian soldiers, Paco had to hire his own armed MP to defend him outside his rented home.

Every day, Paco was required to be at the government offices to be interrogated and every day he was sent home. The routine was maddening. He really felt like each official was taking his turn trying to wear him down. When he was not with the military personnel being interrogated, he was at the Chase Manhattan Bank trying to get a cashier's check cashed. Until the cashier's check was cashed, he was very low on funds.

The days turned into weeks and the weeks turned into months. Finally, after Paco had been in Liberia for more than two months, he was sent to wait in line for his cashier's check to be cashed. The bank was an extremely busy place with hundreds of people passing through every hour. On this particular day, Paco took his place in line, thrilled to finally be closer to receiving his long-awaited cash. The line was very long. The wait was irritating. To make time pass faster, he decided to make small talk with the man ahead of him in line.

"Hi," Paco ventured. "Where are you from?"

"The states," the man answered matter-of-factly.

"Really? So am I. Whereabouts in the states?"

"Texas. How about you?"

"I'm from Texas, too," Paco replied. "Where in Texas?"

"Dallas. How about you?"

"I'm from Dallas, too!" Paco said. "What are you doing here?"

"I am mining for gold."

"Interesting," Paco exclaimed. "So am I. Who is your geologist?"

When the man told Paco who his geologist was, he was amazed. The man was using our geologist. Finally, Paco asked him where he was mining. He was mining on our property. As it turned out, when Paco was put under tight surveillance and had been restricted from setting up his mining operations, our geologist had re-sold our claims to this man, using the same Liberian partner. Paco and his new friend exchanged cards and vowed to see one another again to swap stories once they both returned to the states.

The Lord had set up a divine appointment for Paco to meet this miner from Dallas. Although he was grateful to the Lord for showing him the truth, Paco was hurt and confused as to why we had been betrayed. Both Paco and I were so impressed with our geologist's credentials. Neither of us could believe a man with such an impressive list of accomplishments in his life would feel the need to lie, cheat and steal in his old age.

"Don't worry about it, sweetie," I said on one of our rare phone calls. The phone service in Liberia was pathetic and out much of the time. When it was in service, we both had to scream into the phone in order to hear each other. "Just do what you have to do to get yourself and your friends home alive."

To make matters worse, when the Liberian soldiers ransacked Paco's headquarters, they had confiscated his passports. Once Paco had cash, he was able to pay all of the necessary fees to get his passports back and to get permission to leave the country. At the end of May, Paco finally returned home to American soil. He had lost over forty pounds and was dark from the hot African sun. I was never so happy to see my husband as I was that day at the airport. When he took me in his arms, I nearly fainted, I was so weak from the stress of it all. It had been a very difficult three months for all of us.

A few weeks after his return, we got a bill for $65,000 for the storage fees for the dock in Liberia. "This is ludicrous," I grumbled in disgust. "There is no way we can afford such an exorbitant amount of money."

Paco moved over to where I was standing, and placed his arm gently over my shoulders. "It is not over yet, honey. I am not about to just stand by and watch the Liberian government confiscate that container. There are three trucks in that container."

"Well, I know, honey. But as mad as I get thinking of them taking our stuff, it makes me even angrier when I think of how you were treated over there. Don't you even think of stepping foot in that country again."

"I do think about it, Vic. I think about it all the time. I am going to find a way to get back over there and get our stuff back. There are other good people I met there with good claims. I am just not willing to walk away from it all just yet."

The three months following Paco's return were very difficult. Within a month after his homecoming, I felt the Lord releasing me to retire the business. Our office lease was about to expire and was up for renewal. We converted our garage to office space so Paco would have a place to work on his graphic design. At the same time, I felt the Lord was calling me home for a season.

Paco often awoke in a cold sweat in the middle of the night with recurring nightmares of his time in Liberia. The flashbacks were unbearable. Although our investors were more than understanding, Paco was determined to find a way to return to Africa and make it right. He just could not cope with the idea of leaving the three trucks sitting on the docks in Liberia.

One morning in late August 1984, we were watching *The 700 Club*. Paco was in the living room in front of the television and I had moved to the kitchen to get something. Pat Robertson and Ben Kinchlow were praying for the viewing audience, when Ben had an unusual word of knowledge from the Lord. Ben said, "There's someone whose eyebrows are knit together in a deep scowl. It has something to do with three trucks. The Lord says, 'Release those trucks to Me. It is time to let them go!'"

"Honey," I yelled out. "That's for you. Receive it in the name of Jesus!"

Paco's arms flew into the air in praise to the Lord. "I do receive it, Lord. I release those trucks to You in the name of Jesus!"

From that day forward, Paco had peace about the lost shipment. Although we were both very disappointed and confused as to why the Lord had led us to attempt a gold mining operation in Liberia, we knew that, regardless of the outcome, we had been obedient to what we believed with all of our heart He had called us to do. Shortly after that, in a discussion over dinner with Pastor Larry and his wife, he assured us that sometimes God calls us to do things that are unsuccessful, to see if we will obey Him the next time He asks us to step out in blind faith and obey Him. We determined then not to fix our eyes on the outcome. If God called us to something, we would obey – regardless of the outcome and regardless of whether or not it made sense.

"...for I have learned how to be content (satisfied to the point where I am not disturbed or disquieted) in whatever state I am. I know how to be abased and live humbly in straitened circumstances, and I know also how to enjoy plenty and live in abundance. I have learned in any and all circumstances the secret of facing every situation, whether well-fed or going hungry, having a sufficiency and enough to spare or going without and being in want. I have strength for all things in Christ who empowers me [I am ready for anything and equal to anything through Him who infuses inner strength into me: I am self-sufficient in Christ's sufficiency]."

Philippians 4:11-13

CHAPTER 7

The Church On The Rock Years

∞

Not long after we settled into our garage office, I made an appointment with our insurance man to stop by for a routine renewal of our life insurance policy. When he came to the door that Monday morning, I was surprised to see his foot in a cast.

"What happened to you, Tommy? Did you break your foot?"

"Well," Tommy said. "I decided to go horseback riding with a group of friends Friday. It has been awhile since I have been up on a horse." He stopped and chuckled good-naturedly. "I guess I am not the equestrian I thought I was. When that horse kicked me off, I was lucky to just break my foot. I am bruised from head to toe. That dang horse really got the best of me."

"Where were you?" I asked. "Were you near a hospital?"

"Yeah, I was in Austin. My friends ran me down to the emergency room. As soon as they could get me in, they took x-rays and saw that I had a bad break in the bone in my foot. It still hurts like heck."

We went over the papers he brought and were finished with the business of renewing our policies fairly quickly. Paco spoke up, as Tommy was getting ready to get up out of his chair and hobble on his "boot" to the door. In a tone of voice that was uncharacteristically animated, he said, "Vic! Tell Tommy about Jonathan and how the Lord healed his eyes. If Jesus can heal Jonathan, he can heal Tommy."

"That's true," I thought. "The Lord is no respecter of persons. What He can do for one, He can do for another."

"Tommy," I said excitedly. "Do you believe the Lord heals people?"

Tommy looked taken aback, but only for a moment. "I do."

I continued on excitedly. "Let me tell you about this little five-year-old boy that came to our house last year. His story is so amazing. It will blow your mind and increase your faith."

I told him of Jonathan and what a wondrous miracle God did in his young life. When I finished speaking, Tommy was enthusiastic.

"Well? What are we waiting for? I am ready."

I jumped up and got my anointing oil, explaining to Tommy what James 5:15 says about praying for the sick. I glanced over at Paco, who was seated behind his desk.

"Extend your arm forth, honey, and believe with me for this, okay? Agree with me that Jesus will heal Tommy's foot." Paco stretched his arm forth in obedience. Tommy closed his eyes and bowed his head.

"Dear Jesus," I prayed. "Please do a creative miracle in Tommy's foot, Lord. He's seen the x-rays and he knows, Lord, that without a creative miracle from You, he's doomed to remain in this cast for a while. You know Tommy, Lord, and You love Tommy. Lord, we pray that right now, in the precious name of Jesus, You would heal Tommy's foot. We believe You for it, Lord. Amen."

Before I could say amen, Tommy was standing to his feet. "I can feel the heat all over my foot, you guys. I am serious. The pain is gone. My foot is fine. It is just fine."

"Tommy," I asked, astonished at his instant miracle. "Are you sure? Can you walk?"

"Can I walk? I can run. I can jump up and down. Praise God, I am healed!"

"Tommy," I said. "Listen to me. This is really important. I want you to do me a favor. I believe it is important to document miracles. Where can you go to get an x-ray today? I want you to go straight from here to get your foot x-rayed." He was pensive for a moment, and then he thought of someone.

"I have a friend," he said, "that is a chiropractor. I am sure I can go get an x-ray from him today."

"Do it, Tommy," I encouraged him. "It is really important that you have medical proof that God healed your foot. It is the only way many people will ever believe you."

"I will go there straight from here," Tommy responded excitedly. Not surprisingly, the x-ray showed a normal bone, with no sign whatsoever of a break. That night, Tommy's father died suddenly of a heart attack. The next time we saw him, he related how much it meant to him, in the center of his sorrow and grief, to know the Lord loved him so much he had healed him physically on a day that was to become one of the most emotionally painful days of his life. **Only God knows what we need. When we need it. And why.**

My faith was once again renewed. Having just witnessed another healing miracle, I wanted to lay hands on everyone I could get my hands on. As a woman's care leader for Church on the Rock, I did not have to look very far. I could not wait to meet to tell them all what was happening. The next meeting I attended was at Linda's house. The minute it seemed appropriate, I began to tell the story of how Tommy had come to the house with a broken foot and left running out the door with his foot fully healed. Everyone's faith was high that night.

"So, if any of you is sick and has a need, let's take it to the Lord now and ask Him to heal you. Who needs to be healed tonight?" Janice, a beautiful woman in her early forties spoke up first.

"I have hypoglycemia. Do you think the Lord can heal me of that?"

"I do not even know what that is, but I know God does. Let's all huddle around Janice and believe God for her healing."

I got out my anointing oil and reminded the Lord of His word in James 5:15, where He tells us to pray for the sick and they will be healed. Janice felt the heat of healing that night, and knew she was healed. The next time we all got together again she gave a testimony of her healing.

"Who else needs to be healed?" I asked with confidence. **"Come drink from the well of life. The Lord wants to meet you**

here tonight."

Anne got up and came over and sat down across from me. "What do you need from the Lord tonight, Anne?" I asked, as I gazed intensely into her cool blue eyes. Anne had a natural beauty that was almost soothing to behold.

"I know this sounds crazy. But I've had corns on my feet for as long as I can remember. I would like the Lord to remove my corns."

"Consider it done, Anne." I commanded the corns to fall off her feet in the name of Jesus. The next time we gathered as a group, Anne testified that when she pulled her socks off that night, the corns had fallen off. Anne was corn free!

I did not have to hear their testimonies to know the Lord had healed the women that were prayed for that night. The intensity I had in my life at that time is hard to explain. I was so focused on the Lord, His Word and prayer. In my spirit, I was convinced that all things were possible to those who believed. The scripture in the Amplified Bible I had read in Isaiah 30:18 came back to me often: "And therefore the Lord waits to be gracious unto you…." He is just waiting for *us*, I often thought. He is just *waiting* to be gracious unto us. It was a wonderful, giddy time in my Christian walk. It had been just two years since I had first prayed out loud. I felt the Lord had grown me up quickly. I was soon to find out, however, that not everyone was pleased with the way the Lord was moving in my life.

The next ladies care group was at Doris' house. Doris was my "touch pastor" – the supervisor over a group of women care leaders. Doris had not been at the meeting we had at Linda's house where everyone was prayed over, but she had already heard many of the testimonies of what happened that night. We were all so excited to be together again, and most of the women had come prepared with new needs they wanted prayed over. They made a line and waited for me to pray over each one of them. Once again, the power of God met us, as we believed in perfect agreement that God could do anything.

It was a dizzying experience I never forgot. The anointing of the Holy Spirit was so heavy that we were all shaking. I had no doubt that every prayer lifted to the throne room of God that night was heard and answered. As I headed for the door, Doris met me there. I was the last one to leave.

"Vicki, I will walk you to the car. I want to talk to you."

As we walked toward my car, I could tell by the tone of her voice she was not pleased. "I want you to discontinue your care groups. I will allow you to pray at the prayer rail when the prayer ministers are called forward at the church services, but I do not want you to have or attend women's care groups." She sounded angry and disgusted.

"Doris," I said quietly. "I honestly do not understand. I believe the Lord is pleased that we are coming to Him and believing Him at His Word."

She held firm in her decision and added, " I think what I just witnessed back there was a one-woman show. It could be called 'The Vicki Garza Show.' As your touch pastor, I have the authority to ask you to refrain from meeting in small groups. Trust me. It is in the best interest of all of us." I was reeling from the severity of what she had just said. Somehow, I found the words to respond to her.

"I understand, Doris. I really do. I understand spiritual authority. I'll do as you ask of me."

As I got in my car and drove away, I fought the hot tears, incredulous at the cruelty of her words. "Why, Lord? Are You displeased with me? I only wanted to bring You glory, Lord. You know I am not self-seeking."

I had peace that the Lord was pleased with me. However, I did feel He called me to submit to my touch pastor. I never told anyone except Paco about the incident. The other women never knew, unless Doris told them, why I did not come back. Reflecting on the incident, I know I must have truly been walking under a mighty anointing from the Lord. In the natural, if I was operating in the flesh, I would have gone to a staff member above Doris and made an issue out of it. However, I knew in my spirit the Lord was calling me to a higher walk. I kept my mouth shut and prayed for Doris. It was the only way I could keep bitterness from building up in my heart toward her.

It was not the last time I would encounter jealousy in the church. I was saddened that the women who had been given titles and ranks in the church felt intimidated by me. By the time the Lord called us to leave the area in 1987, I had encountered several other female leaders who were threatened by God's call on my life and asked me to discontinue my ministry. Each time, I did as they asked without question, and refrained from my work in the Lord.

I was certain that God had called me to Church on the Rock to be a lay minister, without title or authority. If and when God chose to promote me was fine with me. If He did not choose to promote me at all, that was fine with me, too. The last thing on my mind was promotion or politics. I did not need to be recognized by the church to have a mission for the Lord. I wanted to worship Him in spirit and in truth. And to know the Lord was pleased with me. In my spirit, I sensed He was.

> *"He said to them, Go into all the world and preach and publish openly the good news (the Gospel) to every creature [of the whole human race]. He who believes [who adheres to and trusts in and relies on the Gospel and Him Whom it sets forth] and is baptized will be saved [from the penalty of eternal death]; but he who does not believe [who does not adhere to and trust in and rely on the Gospel and Him Whom it sets forth] will be condemned. And these attesting signs will accompany those who believe: in My name they will drive out demons; they will speak in new languages; they will pick up serpents; and even if they drink anything deadly, it will not hurt them; they will lay their hands on the sick, and they will get well. So then the Lord Jesus, after He had spoken to them, was taken up into heaven and He sat down at the right hand of God. And they went out and preached everywhere, while the Lord kept working with them and confirming the message by the attesting signs and miracles that closely accompanied [it]. Amen [so be it]."*
>
> *Mark 16:15-20*

CHAPTER 8

My Old Chap

Christmas Day, 1985, I awoke to the sounds of my three small children pleading with me in unison to open just one present before we came out to film Christmas morning at the Garza house. It was a familiar scene by now and had become an annual tradition to allow the children one gift to play with, while mommy and daddy prepared for the big morning. As I laid there that morning, I crossed my arms behind my head and stared at the ceiling, remembering the hot August night my Dad had called and told me about the vision he had experienced while my Mom was in Dallas visiting our family.

"Hey, Dad. How are you doing? We had a great time with Mom the past few days. I imagine you really missed her." Dad was strangely silent, as I fired questions at him about his week without Mom. Finally, I stopped talking and asked if he was okay. It was unlike him to be so quiet with me.

"Yeah, Vic, I am okay. I guess. Promise you won't think I am crazy? Some really strange things have been happening here while your Mom was down visiting you. It all started Thursday night...."

I listened intently as my Father told of his unusual meeting with the Full Gospel Businessmen Fellowship International. There was a guest speaker from Norwich, England, speaking that night. After he spoke, he invited people to come forward for prayer. Dad's heart started beating fast and loud, and he heard the Holy Spirit tell him to go forward for prayer. He had asked this man to pray for him for guidance.

In the early hours of the morning on Saturday, my Dad had a vision. It was a very vivid image of an apple tree. The branches were strong and healthy, and it was heavily laden with fruit. My Dad's eyes traveled down to the roots, and to his amazement, they were completely rotted. "What does this mean?" my Father asked the Lord. Then there was a new vision in front of him. The old stump, with the rotted roots zoomed up close, and he saw a tender, green shoot growing off to the right of the stump.

The Lord answered him: "You are the branches. Your saved children are the fruit. You are all healthy, as you have the life-giving blood of Jesus Christ. The roots are your ancestors. Once vibrant with the blood of Jesus, the living ones are now dead to His voice. The green shoot is the one that is not. Go back to your homeland. Find your living ancestors. Tell them of the true gospel of Jesus Christ."

"I can understand how shook up you must have been, Dad. That is some vision."

"That is not all of it. You won't believe what happened next."

"You mean there is more?" I asked.

He had my full attention as he explained that Sunday morning, he went out to walk around the backyard, as he often did. Only this day, there was something different. He walked over to the old apple tree, and stood in astonishment at the place where it had once been. In its place was an old stump, the roots rotted away. Lying on the ground was a healthy looking tree, loaded with apples! This was tangible evidence that his vision really was from God. After all, the demise of this tree was completely contrary to nature.

"So," Dad concluded, "that is what has been going on up here."

"What are you going to do, Dad?"

"We are going to England to find our living ancestors."

"What do you mean, when you say 'we?'"

"You and me, Vic. After all, you are the one who found the old family Bible and got all of the rest of us interested in our ancestors. Ask Paco if he will let you go."

And so, I had asked Paco. He said he did not mind at all, as long as it was during a time that he could take the kids to his parents' house in Mexico. Christmas through New Years seemed to be the best time. And now, the big day was here.

"I wonder if we will find anyone," I thought, as I climbed out of bed.

"Mommy, Mommy! Come look at what we got!" My mind snapped back to my children, full of anticipation for Christmas morning. In truth, I could not even begin to imagine the adventure the Lord had in store for me and for my Dad. The story is so amazing, I have never told it to anyone but Paco.

The next day, as we were departing the plane, I looked over at Dad. He did not look too much better than I felt. All night in a jumbo jet can really be the pits. Neither one of us had gotten a drop of sleep. Here it was, 4:30 in the morning, New York time, and in London it was 9:30 a.m.

We boarded a bus and rode for a long time. Finally, the bus came to a halt. As everyone began to file out, I looked around. All I saw in front of me was an old prop plane. Surely, they did not intend for us to get on that!

"Are you going to get on that plane, Dad?"

"Yep," Dad beamed confidently. "It looks like this is our ride to Norwich."

As we boarded the small aircraft, I could not help but wonder: "What was I doing here, anyway?" Once the plane took off, it was not that bad.

"Look, Vic." I felt my Dad's elbow poke my ribs.

I had never seen anything like it. It was a perfectly formed round rainbow, brilliant in color, visible out our left window. The shadow of the plane was perfectly centered in the circle of the rainbow, and never did move out of the center of it. I looked away for a second, and when I looked back, a second circle had formed around the first one. It was just a touch lighter in hue, but it was a perfect double round rainbow just the same.

"What do you think it means, Dad? Do you think the Lord is telling us we are in the center of His perfect will?"

"I don't know, Vic. I don't know. Listen, don't tell anybody. They will never believe you."

After landing, and after we had adjusted to getting into the wrong side of the car and driving on the wrong side of the road, we went directly to our hotel. The rest of the afternoon was spent recuperating from our jet lag, and plotting our course of action. Dad had given me the name of a genealogist in Norwich that a friend of his had found in an old magazine. I had contacted him before the trip, and we had arranged a meeting for that day.

Later on that afternoon, Patrick Palgrave-Moore arrived. He was the epitome of class – a perfectly proper Englishman. "Oh boy, is he in for a treat. He has probably never seen the likes of us," I chuckled to myself. "What must he think…an old farmer and his daughter, looking for their long-lost relatives in Norwich, England?" I could just imagine how odd it must have looked.

Saturday morning came quickly. Patrick had been very helpful and instructed us to convert our dollars into pounds as soon as possible. We pulled into a parking lot downtown, and asked the attendant if he could point us in the direction of the nearest bank. Detecting our accent, he asked us where we were from. As soon as we explained what we were doing in Norwich, he urged us to run into the radio station across the street and ask for "Wally". He was the announcer for Radio Norfolk. The attendant explained that most of Norwich and the surrounding towns listened to that station. More than likely, one of our long-lost relatives would be listening and would respond.

Within minutes, a pleasant Englishman by the name of Wally was interviewing me. The taped interview was played that day and the next. Just as we had hoped, a lovely family called in that evening to say they were fairly certain they were related to us.

That Saturday, we experienced so many miraculous events it boggled our minds. Incredibly, we found Westfield (it was not even on the map), the town where Robert Miller, our original English ancestor, was born, converted to Christianity and married. We visited the old parish church and stood outside the house that had once been his home in the early 1800's. We were incredulous, as we moved from one town to the next, finding exactly that for which we were looking.

From there, we went to Runhall, where George and Alice Bowles had lived. We spied a couple walking down the lane, and asked them if they happened to know of a family by the name of Bowles. They apologetically explained that they owned a vacation home in Runhall, and knew very few people. They did, however, know a man that was very familiar with the historical records of the town. They invited us into their home for tea, while they tried to find him for us. While they were looking for their friend, we decided to visit the Runhall parish church where Brother Bowles had probably preached. It was a wonderfully quaint structure with many of the old fixtures and books still intact. After visiting the church, we went back to the couple's home for a cup of tea and to meet their friend who had the information we were seeking.

Soon after we arrived, a short, stocky, elderly man entered. He introduced himself and asked us what it was we would like to know. We explained that we were interested in a family by the name of Bowles, who had originated from the area. His eyes lit up as he recognized the name.

Coincidentally, a woman by the name of Bowles had lived in that very house. As a boy, he remembered Widow Bowles well. She had told him how the house had stayed in the family since the early 1800's, when a primitive Methodist preacher named Bowles had lived there and preached in the small chapel that was attached to the house. He showed us the dining room, and explained how that once was a chapel. It had been cut in half to make a dining room for the cottage as well as a garage. The garage still had the original chapel ceiling in it.

We shared with them what we knew of the Bowles family that had come to America, and then asked if they would like to hear their obituaries. As I sat before the blazing fire and read the powerful Christian testimony of the man who had once occupied that room, my heart bowed in awe to my magnificent Maker. I knew I would never again limit Him, nor question His ability to order our steps.

This is the obituary written about Rev. George Bowles in 1884 that I read in his family home in Runhall. I found it in the old family Bible in April 1983, when I had flown home to New York to visit Grandma Ann in the hospital. Before that, none of us had any idea that our ancestors were powerful, praying Christians.

"Rev. George Bowles passed to his reward in Plains, NY, on

April 16, 1884. He was born in Fellthorp, England, March 13, 1809, and was married to Alice Adcock in July 1828. He was rescued from a wicked course of life by God's grace, and happily converted. The love of Christ was shed abroad richly in his heart, and permeated his entire being. Brother Bowles preached and prayed with power. In 1852, he was ordained deacon. The widow and the orphan found in him a constant friend. In the midst of temptation, he was unmurmuring, and always had a good word for the sorrowing. He was ill for two weeks. Loved ones stood around his bed, eager to catch his last words. He exclaimed, 'Hallelujah! Almost home!' and triumphantly passed away. He has left a widow and nine children, but they sorrow not as those who have no hope. They anticipate a reunion in heaven. Until then, they will enjoy the heritage left them by the memory of the devoted and useful life of their departed loved one, for it is written, 'the memory of the just is blessed and the righteous shall be an everlasting remembrance.'"

Even as I read it aloud to our new friends, I was reminded of the fact that obituaries were once such a powerful witnessing tool.

"I say, love. Where to for dinner?" my Father quipped in his newfound accent.

"Wherever you say, old chap," I answered. I could not believe that all we had eaten all day was a "sweet" and a cup of tea. It was after 6:00 already. "How about Cromer? According to our book, that has excellent seafood."

So Cromer it was.

Halfway to Cromer, I strained my eyes to make out what looked like a person lying on the side of the road.

"Stop, Dad!" I yelled. There was a man lying there, with his bicycle sprawled out beside him. A woman was holding his head up, but obviously, medical help had not yet arrived. We went running over to him and knelt down beside him.

"What happened? Are you hurt badly? Has someone called an ambulance?" My heart went out to him. He said he had been there for hours before this woman had finally stopped to help. He could not move his leg and was sure it was broken. The pain was unbearable. He told me he was from Norway, his name was Glenn Matthiason, and that it was his 18th birthday.

"Glenn Matthiason," I said. "I am going to pray for you and ask the Lord Jesus to heal your leg." As I knelt over his leg, I prayed in the spirit. Laying my hands on his knee and calf, I felt the healing virtue of the Lord being released like a hot salve upon his body. "How does your leg feel now, Glenn?" I asked confidently.

"Great. I think I can walk on it!" Without further adieu, he hopped up and started walking in a circle. Just then, the ambulance arrived. Dad and I quietly walked back to our car, and drove off for Cromer. We were both silent for a few moments, as we considered the awesome thing the Lord had just done. I could not help but meditate on the scripture in Isaiah 30:18, where the Lord says He is waiting for *us*.

Sunday morning came quickly. The dinner the night before had been delightful and we had slept soundly. We had a full day planned. A church had been recommended to us and then we were going to John Wright's home for lunch. He was the director for the Full Gospel Businessman's Fellowship International in Norwich. After lunch we headed out to meet the relatives that had found us via the radio interview taped the day before. It was a full day, but nowhere near as exciting as Saturday had been.

Back in the room Monday night, we discussed the day. We had just come back from eight hours of visually scanning public records in the local library, and I was exhausted. We had not been able to find any other relatives living in England, or to verify that the ones we had met on Sunday were related. My head pounded and my back ached. I was chilled to the bone.

"Well, Dad, don't you think our mission was accomplished? After all, we did find some people that are most likely related to us. Too bad we never got to tell them about Jesus."

"They were wonderful people, Vic, but I just do not think they are the ones we were sent here to find. There has to be someone else. We were sent here specifically for someone who has been praying for the Lord to reveal Himself to them."

Suddenly, everything looked so bleak. Here it was Monday night and tomorrow was New Year's Eve. The day after that, we were leaving for London and then home. I sat on the bed massaging my cold toes, trying to bring some life back into them. It was nearly

7:30, and we had not even eaten dinner. Dad was insisting that we drag ourselves back out into the miserable weather to go to Patrick's house. He had invited us over to discuss the findings of the day. Ugh! All I wanted to do was take a hot bath and crawl into bed. As Dad pulled me out the door, a now familiar thought was ringing in my ears: "What was I doing here, anyway?"

"Oh, it was so wonderful to speak with you on the phone, Vicki!" Sylvia exclaimed with genuine excitement. Sylvia was Patrick's wife. She was being such a gracious hostess to us, I felt ashamed for wanting to stay behind in the hotel room. Poor Patrick was lost amid a stack of notes I had taken earlier in the day and was patiently transcribing them. "I remember that morning you called, Vicki. Your voice sounded like it was just next-door. It was 11:30 in the morning here. What time was it in Dallas?" When I told her it was 5:30 a.m., she gasped in surprise. "What on earth were you doing up at 5:30 in the morning?" My mind raced to give her an answer.

"Oh, what the heck," I thought. "This whole episode is about at a close, anyway. I may as well be honest with her. "Because of our impending trip, I was getting up every morning at 4:30 to pray for an hour."

Her response was sincere and immediate. "Oh, how absolutely wonderful! Tell me, could you explain the passage of scripture where…."

I could not believe my ears. This dear woman was incredibly thirsty for enlightenment concerning the Bible. I told her of my father's vision and exactly why we had come to England to find our living relatives. She listened entranced as the rest of the story of our trip unfolded. When I was finished, she turned to Patrick, who was still engrossed in his notes. "Do you know, dear, I believe my Aunt Daisy was a Bowles." Patrick slowly put his papers down beside him. "Your Aunt Daisy, a Bowles, you say?" For a moment there was complete silence. Then my Dad shot up off of the couch where we were sitting. "You are the shoot!" he shouted, remembering that tender green shoot in his vision from the Lord.

Back in the room that night, we were both elated. It was 2:00 a.m., and we had just gotten in from Patrick and Sylvia's home. We sat up for quite awhile, talking and re-living the past six hours. Who would have ever thought that the genealogist we had hired would turn out to be the very one the Lord had sent us for? He and Sylvia were both so hungry for spiritual answers. It felt so good to know that the very thing we had been sent to do, we had accomplished. We both wondered how long it would take Patrick to verify that we were truly related to Sylvia.

Tuesday morning came way too fast. After seeing Fellthorp, the birthplace of my Dad's Great Grandfather George Bowles, we decided to venture out to a place on the map that had caught my Father's eye. There were four corners out in the middle of nowhere that had a circle around it. Neither of us had put it there. It looked as though it had been printed there, but I could not find a symbol like that on the map legend. After making many turns onto one country lane after another, Dad stopped the car. "Well," he announced triumphantly, "looks like this is it."

I looked around, wondering why on earth the Lord had led us on this wild goose chase. Just as I was about to suggest we had made a mistake, Dad spoke up. "Look, Vic. Here comes an old lady. Ask her if anyone by the name of Bowles has ever lived around here."

"Bowles, you say? Do you mean George Bowles? The old man George Bowles lived right there in that little white cottage for years." My hair stood right up on my neck, as I looked at the white cottage. It was sitting at the four corners marked on the map. She continued, "He just died a few years ago at the age of 101. His son lives in Kensington, Surrey, in London."

As our car pulled away, I picked the map back up to look at the circle. It was as though the blinders had been removed from my eyes, as I exclaimed to Dad, "You are never going to believe this! That "O" was the "O" in the county of N-O-R-F-O-L-K!"

Wednesday morning, New Year's Day, we had not made any plans, other than our train trip to London later on in the day. I was propped up in bed reading to Dad out of the Hebrew Greek Study Bible he had gotten just before the trip.

"Hey, Dad, this is neat. I always wondered what Hebrews 6:1-6 meant. It says here that your repentance must be acceptable unto God...." I continued to read the two pages of footnotes that explained the verses. When I had finished, Dad looked at me. I could tell he had something on his mind.

"Do you think Patrick is home?"

"I don't know, Dad. It is New Year's Day. Why do you ask?"

"I want to give him and Sylvia that study Bible."

Patrick escorted us in. He seemed so serious as he went over and sat down in his old chair by the fire. "It seems we are related, Bob," he said to my Dad. "Aunt Daisy was not a Bowles. Her name was Boley. However, as I traced Sylvia's lines back, I discovered that five generations back, she came from Frances Bowles, who married Joseph Blower in 1810."

He handed us the information he had gathered. How very strange, I thought to myself. The one she thought was a Bowles was not. But there was a Bowles in her lineage anyway. That was mind-boggling. As we presented Patrick and Sylvia with their Bible, they seemed pleased, yet disturbed, as my Dad explained to them that the Lord had heard their pleas for help and had sent us all the way across the Atlantic Ocean to England, just for them. As our car headed out, I turned back to wave one last time to our new relatives.

"I say, love, where to?" my Dad chided.

"Where else, old chap? London!"

At breakfast Thursday morning, we were both caught up in our own thoughts. I was thinking about the church we had visited New Year's Eve and the new friends we had made there. After several minutes, my mind began to wander to other thoughts.

"You know, Dad, I wonder which of the seven churches described in Revelation represents the evangelical church in England."

Dad said, "You know, Vic, I've been hearing the Holy Spirit telling me to read the first four chapters of Revelation for days now. I guess we had better go up to the room and read it."

This time, Dad read to me, while I filed my nails. He was in the fourth chapter: "…And behold, a throne was set in heaven…and there was a rainbow round about the throne…" I spun around in my seat to look at him, then immediately threw my hands up in the air to praise the Lord of heaven and earth.

"Thank you, Lord," I shouted. "I knew you would explain that round rainbow to me."

Later, I exclaimed: "Hey, Dad. I found him!" I turned to close the door of the phone booth behind me. "I spoke with George Bowles' son. He was one of the four Bowles that was listed in Kensington, Surrey. He said his mother and father live close by him, and that he would tell them that we will be there at 5:00 this afternoon."

My Dad just shook his head. "We should know by now that the Lord could do anything, shouldn't we?"

We went back to the hotel to prepare for our meeting with George Bowles, the son of the man who had lived in the little white cottage at the four corners in the middle of nowhere.

Of course, we did meet George Bowles and his wife, Lily, that night. They were delightful. Although they were well into their 80s, they were so full of life and charm. We were not able to tell them, however, the true purpose of our trip. We left there more convinced than ever that our mission had been accomplished the first night we spent at Patrick's house.

It was wonderful to meet and speak with people who were our blood relatives. But most rewarding of all was the knowledge we had done that which the Lord had asked us to do. We had set out for England in blind faith, believing the Lord would fulfill His promise to us.

In turn, the Lord had indeed fulfilled his scriptural promise to us from Isaiah 30:18 (the Amplified Bible): He was faithful to show us His love, His peace, His joy and His matchless, unbroken companionship.

"Believe Me that I am in the Father and the Father in Me, or else believe Me for the sake of the [very] works themselves. [If you cannot trust Me, at least let these works that I do in My Father's name convince you]. I assure you, most solemnly I tell you, if anyone steadfastly believes in Me, he will himself be able to do the things that I do; and he will do even greater things than these, because I go to the Father. And I will do [I myself will grant] whatever you ask in My name [as presenting all that I Am], so that the Father may be glorified and extolled in

(through) the Son. [Yes] I will grant [I Myself will do for you] whatever you shall ask in My name [as presenting all that I Am]."

John 14:11-15

CHAPTER 9

Called Cross-Country

❧

1986 literally flew by. Paco and I were very involved in our church and with the care group that met just a few houses down from ours. Although I was no longer holding women's care groups in my home, I continued to pray at the altar of the church with people as they came forward to seek the Lord. Frequently I stayed late and prayed with those that were hurting in our community care group. The Lord continued to honor our faith. It seemed we were all walking out the New Testament church.

From that day to this, I have not known or seen the level of anointing that fell upon the congregation of Church on the Rock in Rockwall, Texas, during those years. Many of those of us who were privileged to worship in such a holy place have had great difficulty finding a church that satisfies the deep longing in our soul for more of the power and love of Jesus in our lives.

One day in late summer 1986, a friend stopped by to chat. She was a friend from church and had grown concerned with certain petty items that were bothering her. I felt myself becoming irritated as she hinted that the church was not the same anymore, now that we were in the midst of a building campaign. "Do you ever think you will leave Church on the Rock, Vicki?"

I looked at her in disbelief. My answer was swift and certain. "No, Laura. As long as we live in Dallas, we will always attend

Church on the Rock. We feel God has planted us there permanently. We love that church."

Even as I said it, I felt a prodding in my spirit. For the first time since attending the church, I had an uneasy premonition that everything was about to change for all of us. Little did I know how accurate a premonition that was. In the fall of 1986, the Holy Spirit had already set the wheels of change in motion.

Paco's youngest brother, Beto, was visiting for a week and they had driven into the city to buy some art supplies for Paco's business. It was a day like any other day, or so I thought. Almost immediately after they left the house, I had a deep stirring in my gut. The pain came deep and low and was unlike anything I had ever felt.

I ran to my room and shut the door. I began to pace the room in anticipation of what the Lord was about to do. I do not know exactly how I knew the ache was from the Lord. But somehow I knew He was about to speak to me in a profound way. After pacing for a few minutes, I walked into our large master bathroom and sat on the floor, rocking.

I stopped praying in the spirit and waited for the Lord to speak to my spirit. When He did speak, the message was short and to the point.

"Vicki, I am about to do a new work in your lives. Prepare your hearts for this new work. I am moving you out in a new walk of faith. Do not fear. I will provide for all of your needs as you walk in obedience to My voice."

"Yes, Lord. Wherever You call us, whatever You require of us, we will obey."

Within moments, the phone rang. It was my dear intercessory prayer partner, Rose. Her Fijian accent was thick as she greeted me. "Vicki," she said with urgency. "Do you have a minute? The Lord is speaking to me about you and Paco and the new plans He has for you. God is going to move you out into a new place. A place you have never walked before. The Lord is showing me that He is pleased with you and that He has a new path He wants to take you down. Has the Lord prepared your heart for this word? Do you receive it as being from the Lord?"

"Rose," I said emphatically. "The Lord has been speaking to my spirit the exact same thing for the past few minutes. I know this is a confirmation that I did hear from the Lord. Thanks for your obedience in calling and sharing what He showed you concerning our lives."

I could hardy wait for Paco to walk in the door. When he did, it would be awhile before I could get him alone to talk to him privately. Finally, we had some time to ourselves. "Sweetie, I have something to tell you."

A look of concern crossed his face. I could tell he thought I was pregnant.

"No, I am not pregnant." I laughed. "We both know we are done having kids. I wanted to tell you something the Lord shared with me while you were gone."

The muscles that had tightened in his face relaxed and he smiled warmly. "Go ahead. I am all ears." As I told him the things the Lord had spoken to me and confirmed through Rose, he listened intently. When I finished, he sat for a moment as though he was choosing his words carefully.

"Exactly what do you think the Lord is asking us to do?"

"I honestly do not know, honey. I will tell you that I definitely got the impression that there are some big changes up ahead for us. I think there will soon be some obstacles in our business and in the Dallas economy. I believe the Lord spoke to forewarn us so that we could prepare and not be caught unaware. Are you willing to go wherever God calls us and do whatever God shows us to do?"

"Of course I am, Vic." Paco sounded agitated, as though I was suggesting he would not obey God. He studied me closely. "Are you? Are you willing to go to Mexico if God calls us there?"

As I gazed into his warm, brown eyes, my heart sunk. I had not even considered that the Lord would be calling me to something as difficult as moving to Mexico. That was the one thing I was unwilling to do when Paco and I were dating. I knew that, culturally, it would be almost impossible for me to be myself. It would be the death of me. By virtue of gender, the women were to be seen and not heard, a pretty adornment on their husband's pedestal.

"Oh God," I thought. "Please do not ask me to go to Mexico to live." Even as I thought it, I knew I had to sell out to the Lord.

Wherever He chose to send us, He would give us the grace to walk it out.

"Well?" Paco insisted. "Would you move to Mexico, Vicki?" My answer was slow and deliberate.

"If God called us to Mexico, I know He would give me the grace to go."

Paco shook his head in amazement. "I never thought I would ever hear you say those words."

I could not believe my own ears. I honestly did not believe I would ever make that concession either. In my heart, I begged God not to call me to make that sacrifice. The last week of October, we packed our three kids up and drove to Monterrey, Mexico, to see if that was God's next stop for our lives.

The trip had proven to be uneventful. The few interviews that Paco was able to secure while we were there were duds. The government and economy in Mexico were lagging. Everyone was complaining about the recession and loss of income. I breathed a huge sigh of relief, knowing that our assignment for the Lord was somewhere in the states.

"But where, Lord? Where are You sending us?" The answer came more quickly than I had suspected it would. We had barely walked through the door, when the phone rang. It was my Mom.

"Vicki! I am glad you are home. Your father and I went looking at doublewide trailers today. Do you really think you and Paco might move up here any time in the near future?" I strained my mind to remember if I had ever even mentioned to her that moving back to North Cohocton was a possibility. I spent the first eighteen years of my life trying to escape that little town. Why on earth would I want to return?

"Mom, did I tell you we were thinking of moving back to New York?"

"No. Not in those exact words. You said you felt God was moving you out of Dallas. I guess I assumed that meant you would be coming up home."

After I hung up with Mom, I searched my heart: "Lord, only you know that, after Mexico, the next most difficult place for me to live would be North Cohocton." I did not mind visiting once or twice a year. But now that I had lived in a major metropolitan area for so long, I could not even begin to imagine living in a small town, just up the street from my parents and brother George and sister Luanne.

Again, I prayed: "God, if this is You, please give me peace in my heart. Make a way where there seems to be no way, Lord. Only You know what You have planned for us. I leave our future in Your wonderful, capable hands. I trust Your wisdom to guide our lives."

Although the Lord had prepared our hearts for change, it came more quickly than we could have imagined. By the end of 1986, Paco's business had tapered off dramatically. It was clear that if we did not make our move quickly, we would head into a downward spiral fast. The last quarter of 1986, the advertising and marketing segment took a significant hit in Dallas, as a real estate, banking and oil crisis brought the city to a screeching halt. Suddenly, all anyone could talk about was the impending doom of the new economic recession. We were thankful the Lord had prepared our hearts for the move. Knowing He would go with us, we anticipated my trip to New York in early January to scout out the Rochester advertising industry to see if they had room for one more talented graphic designer and illustrator.

In January 1987, I made my move. As I traveled to my parents' home in Upstate New York to look for job opportunities for Paco, I prayed the Lord would meet us in our job search. I knew that without God's intervention in our lives, we were sunk. Where our next job was going to come from, only God knew.

I found the key where my sister, Marcia, had left it for me under the mat at her home in the city. As I let myself into her house to make phone calls to advertising agencies in Rochester, I laid my Bible down next to the yellow pages.

"Lord Jesus," I pleaded, "only You can know how lost I feel right now. Paco and I do not know anyone in Rochester. You know whom You have chosen to use to bless us with work. I beg of You, Lord, please lead me to them this morning."

I had rarely felt so lost. It had been over four years since we had been completely broke, with no hope of income in sight, and the Lord had delivered us in a single sale.

After I prayed, I felt the feeling of depression and hopelessness lifting off of my spirit. "Okay, Lord. It is just You and me," I reminded Him as I opened the phone book to the Advertising Agencies listed for Rochester.

"Show me who You want me to call."

I waited and continued to pray in the spirit until I got a witness to move forward. Finally, my eyes landed on a company called ICE Communications, and I knew I was to start my search there. Armed with pen and paper, I dialed the number. The receptionist put me through to the creative director, a great guy that seemed quite happy to help in any way he could. "No, we don't have any openings. But I'd be happy to give you some names and agencies to call. I can tell you the names of the hottest agencies in town and who you will need to ask for when you call."

"This guy must be my personal angel," I thought, as I quickly jotted down the names of the top agencies in town and their creative directors. His help was invaluable. Within fifteen minutes, I had filled my schedule with portfolio interviews for the next day and a half. I knew in my spirit the Lord was indeed with me and would stay right beside me, as I headed out for my interviews.

The first three interviews I had were pretty routine. The fourth interview, I sensed as I walked through the doors, would prove to be a divine appointment. I sat waiting for the creative director in the conference room, praying under my breath for favor. "Let me be surrounded by Your shield of favor, Lord," I prayed as I waited. Finally, a nice looking, middle-aged man walked through the door and introduced himself. He was congenial and warm and immediately put me at ease. About halfway into the interview, he pulled the portfolio closer to himself to view the detail in Paco's illustration samples. I instinctively moved my chair back, breathing an inward sigh of relief at his obvious approval of Paco's work.

Just then, I experienced one of the strangest things I had ever seen. I saw a soft ray of light resting on his head. I looked up to see if there was a skylight or some other way to explain the light. There was no logical explanation for the beam of light. It literally came out of nowhere. As I was studying him and the light that rested on him, he seemed to be in a world of his own.

"Your husband's work is remarkable, Vicki. His breadth of styles is uncanny. I am amazed at his talent. I feel honored to discover such a talented designer and illustrator. Did you say he is moving to Rochester? How soon can he get here? I would love to be able to hire him to work on some of our advertising campaigns. We are really busy right now and could use him as soon as he can get up here."

And so, just like that, our prayers were answered. I promised him I would get Paco to Rochester as soon as we could make arrangements. He promised to have a furnished office waiting for him. To start with the agency, Paco would have to remain self-employed. Once he proved himself, they would hire him on full time.

The next few weeks were packed with excitement as Paco and I prepared for his move to New York. He would live with my parents until the kids and I could join him there. We agreed that the end of May would probably work best, since that was when school finished for our kids in Dallas. Toward the end of February, Paco stood by his packed car, ready to make the cross-country trip by himself.

As he hugged and kissed me and tousled three-year old David's hair, he called to our resident hawk, which often hovered over the forest across the street. From nowhere, the hawk appeared and answered him, swooping in front of us, and then quickly lifting himself high above the woods.

"We will take that as a sign, darling, that the Lord will be with you," I choked tearfully. Then Paco got into his little Nissan and drove off for New York.

The next three months were very difficult times for me. I was stretched to capacity with three small children to attend to. I had the pressure of preparing for the move alone. In addition to looking for tenants to rent out our own home, our other rental home had opened up for a May renter, after three years with the same wonderful tenant.

However, as difficult as the stress and pressure was financially and physically, I was unprepared for the emotional distress of raising three small children alone in a "couples" society. I developed a very strong empathy for single moms during that time. I felt like a single mom in every way, other than the long-distance emotional support I got from Paco. Although I had been attending the church for years, it suddenly seemed like all of my married friends were avoiding any close contact with me. It was a very strange sensation to feel the rejection of being single. It definitely contributed to my loneliness during that time. If it had not been for my dear friends Bruce and Rose, who came and called to see if I needed anything, I would have felt totally rejected by my own. To this day, I have a soft spot in my heart for both singles and single parents. It can be a very lonely life.

Just before I was to leave for my move to New York, my friend Rose shared with me what she had seen in the spirit. She and her husband Bruce had come over to help me pack. They were also leaving for an extended time in Fiji.

"Vicki," she said in her strong Fijian accent, "I have something to tell you. I was praying for you today and I had a vision of you. You were pregnant. The Lord told me you are going to have more children."

"Rose," I responded in a soft, condescending voice. I wanted to show her respect yet let her know she must be mistaken. "Paco and I are finished having children. If you saw me pregnant in a vision, I must have been pregnant in the spirit. Maybe I am going to birth something in the spirit."

She shook her head from side to side emphatically. I could tell she was not budging. "I tell you, Vicki. Mark my words. You and Paco are going to have more children. You will see. The Lord has more boys to give you."

I called a truce and gave her a big hug. I held her tight and thanked the Lord for giving me such a wonderful friend. My eyes filled with tears as she and Bruce pulled away from the curb and I watched their car disappear around the corner. "God speed, my friends," I prayed in a whisper. I was not sure if I would ever see them again.

Six weeks after Paco left for New York State, I found myself in the principal's office of the school, begging her to allow Elisa to leave her second grade classroom for a week of vacation in South Padre Island with her daddy. We had not seen Paco in six weeks and would not see him for at least another seven. He had arranged to come home to Texas the week between Palm Sunday and Easter, since that was the week his parents would be staying in South

Padre. It was important to Paco that we all connect one last time with his folks before moving so far away.

Sitting in the principal's office, it was unfathomable to me that she would not allow Elisa to leave school for one week to be with her father, who she had not seen in so long. "What do you suggest I do?" I asked through terse lips. I could feel my face flushing and the heat in my body was rising.

"Actually," she replied curtly, "I am certain you must have someone you can leave Elisa with while the rest of your family goes to South Padre for a week. Can you think of someone she would feel comfortable staying with for that week?"

I could not believe my ears. Her lack of understanding was unconscionable. How could she be so callous as to expect us to leave Elisa in Dallas while we all went with her daddy to South Padre Island? My blood was boiling.

"Elisa is at the top of her grade. She can finish a week's worth of class work in one afternoon. I can assure you that she can afford to miss one week of second grade. Please make an exception and allow Elisa to spend that week with her daddy."

I held my breath as I awaited her answer. I did not have to wait long. Her answer was immediate and deliberate. "Absolutely not, Mrs. Garza. I refuse to allow Elisa to take one more week of school. She already lost a week the last week of October. She is not allowed, by Texas State Law, to lose another week."

Sitting across from her desk, I was shaking with anger and disgust. The thought that this woman was in charge of my children's education sickened me. I was certain she could make an exception if she had wanted to. A sense of righteous indignation came over me. Finally, with an air of absolute authority, I spoke in a hushed tone.

"Thank you for your time. I have decided to withdraw my children from your care. I can tell, from our conversation today, you do not have the best interest of my children at heart. The very thought of leaving Elisa here while we all go with her father on vacation, after not seeing him for six weeks, knowing we won't see him for another seven, is ludicrous. I have decided to homeschool my children and will be taking them home with me now."

The principal did not seem the least bit taken aback. She did not even flinch. It seemed to me she had a heart of stone. Her lack of empathy only strengthened my resolve. I was glad I had the moral and spiritual fortitude to stand firm. As I loaded Jessica and Elisa into the car, I was already questioning the wisdom of what I had done. Now what was I going to do? I could not even imagine staying home all day, teaching my children. I had always been the one who felt so comfortable in the workforce, working outside the home since I was a fourteen-year old girl.

"Oh Lord," I prayed. "Please help me do this. I have a feeling this will be the hardest thing I have ever done." Over the next few months, I prayed daily for His grace and wisdom as I set about to teach my three-, five- and seven-year old children at home.

Years later, when I saw her again, the Lord showed me clearly that He had hardened her heart to fulfill His purposes in our lives. As I thanked her silently, I knew in my heart that she had unknowingly done our family a huge favor.

> *"So, too, the [Holy] Spirit comes to our aid and bears us up in our weakness; for we do not know what prayer to offer nor how to offer it worthily as we ought, but the Spirit Himself goes to meet our supplication and pleads in our behalf with unspeakable yearnings and groanings too deep for utterance. And He who searches the hearts of men knows what is in the mind of the [Holy] Spirit [what His intent is], because the Spirit intercedes and pleads [before God] in behalf of the saints according to and in harmony with God's will. We are assured and know that [God being a partner in their labor] all things work together and are [fitting into a plan] for good to and for those who love God and are called according to [His] design and purpose."*
> *Romans 8:26-28*

CHAPTER 10

Lives Changed By God's Power

~

We pulled into North Cohocton the first week of June 1987. It was eerie to be back in my childhood home, living as an adult with a family of my own. Those were giddy days, as we settled into the1850's farmhouse I had grown up in, painting walls and sewing balloon curtains throughout.

Soon after we had moved in, some new church friends, Bill and Kim, shared their farm animal supply with us. Before we knew it, we had a small farm of our own that included several rabbits, a hen, a rooster and a barn cat named Butter. Paco built the children a tree swing that hung from a high branch on a tall pine tree in our back-yard. The children rode their bikes freely around town and down to the same playground I had played on as a child.

Our lives resembled a Norman Rockwell setting. Before long, we were planting and harvesting tomatoes, zucchini and cantaloupes from our own vegetable garden. As the children and I settled into our schooling routine, and Paco settled into his art director's job at the agency, our former life in Dallas seemed like a distant dream.

One day in September, my Mom called to ask me if I would like to go see Miller, my Dad's elderly cousin that was in a nursing home in a nearby town, on the way to the airport to pick up my Father. My Dad was flying in from a mission trip to Israel he had attended with Jimmy Swaggart's ministry team.

I had met Miller just once, the day my Dad and I had flown in from the trip to England. He had a very well-appointed apartment in Rochester, in an old, prestigious mansion in the city. Once a plant manager for the local Birds Eye food processing business, he was still a very poised, professional gentleman. At the age of 86, I was very impressed with his reserved and cultured demeanor. It was obvious by the way he carried himself he had once been a very successful man and had commanded a great deal of respect.

I was surprised to hear he was in a nursing home. I could not imagine how he could have gone downhill so quickly since we had first visited him nearly two years ago. I did not hesitate when Mom called. Of course I would like to go with her to the nursing home to visit him. After all, even though I had just recently met him, he was still my second cousin.

When Mom and I got to Miller's room, I was shocked to see his condition. This man, who had been so in control of his life, was just a shadow of his former self. He complained of pain and suffering from the moment we entered the room until the moment we prepared to leave.

My Mom had been sitting beside him talking, holding his hand, while I sat across the room from them, just listening the entire time. When I did speak, it was as I was leaving. I stopped by him just before I left, to tell him I hoped he would soon be feeling better. Just then, I had a witness in my spirit to pray for him.

"Miller," I said, "would you mind if I pray for you to be healed before I leave? I have seen the Lord heal people. I know He can heal you. Can I pray for you?" Miller nodded his head.

"Please do," he replied weakly.

I laid my hands on his body and prayed for the Lord to meet him at the point of his need and give him a miracle. Mom stood on the other side of him, praying in agreement with me. Then we left, totally unaware of how magnificently God had met Miller's needs that day. It was not until a few months later, when I received a personal, handwritten note from Miller, that I discovered that God had healed Miller completely.

Just a few years ago, my Mom gave me a lengthy testimony

Miller had written shortly after God touched him. He wanted to share the experience with friends and family. He entitled his four-page testimony, *"It is No Secret What God can do."*

In his testimony, he tells about how a bad cold he caught in mid-March quickly progressed into a serious case of pneumonia. For weeks, he had lain unconscious in the hospital, and for months after that he had never gotten out of bed or dressed. He experienced horrible nightmares during that time and thought he was being tortured day and night. He described what horrible pain he was in continually and that he had prayed at least a dozen times a day to die. In mid-July, he moved to the nursing home for financial reasons, and started the long road to recovery.

Miller wrote the following words to tell of his healing experience: "When Alverna and Vicki stopped in to see me (9/1/87), Vicki asked me if I wanted her to pray for me. I said, 'Yes.' She got down on her knees, took both of my hands in hers, closed her eyes and prayed earnestly for half an hour. (I think Miller's concept of time was off here!) Among other things, she said, 'Lord, we expect a miracle. We want Miller's arthritis cured completely. We ask in Jesus' name.' At the same time, Dr. Hayes changed the pain pill. Almost immediately, all pain was gone. I wasn't sure if it was the drug or the prayer that accomplished this. I knew that many people had been praying for my recovery, but this was different. It seemed that Vicki was talking to God standing beside her. From that day on, I got better and better, every day in every way, not only physically, but also mentally. Now (11/8/87) I look forward to waking up every morning and plan to enjoy the day God has made for me."

Once again, it moved me to see how God had touched Miller so powerfully and I did not even realize it. From my mere human viewpoint, I was tired of hearing him complain and anxious to leave to pick up my Dad from the airport. On my way out the door, almost as an afterthought, I asked Miller if he would like me to pray for him. I was not feeling particularly prayed up or prepared to pray for his healing. I just knew that prayer was a courtesy I had to extend to him and I did believe with all of my being that if it was God's will, He could heal Miller. I believe my Mom and Miller also had great faith for his healing. For Miller, **it changed his whole**

world from night to light.

I later learned from my parents that Miller's remaining years on earth were very fruitful. Although I did not stay in touch with him, he had many friends and family members that visited his room. He was always quick to share his healing testimony, as well as the good news of salvation, to all who would listen.

A local, visiting pastor became very close to Miller over time. Sensing that his funeral would be well attended, it was Miller's desire to choose the songs and prepare his own sermon. When the time came, just as Miller had anticipated, hundreds came from miles around to his funeral service. Miller preached the message of hope and salvation from his grave, to a captive audience of friends and loved ones. My parents attended and said they had never witnessed such a powerful funeral service. The pastor preached a lengthy sermon and at Miller's request, an altar call was given. Several came forward, touched by the power of the Holy Spirit. Once again, the Lord had met and exceeded all of our expectations.

The fall of 1987 was a powerful time in my life spiritually. I was privileged to meet an old American Indian by the name of Bob Wittcop at the Full Gospel Businessman's meeting in Bath. Bob was a fascinating old man who lived in the VA Hospital in Bath and never missed a meeting. My Dad and I were intrigued by him and by his amazing life stories. He had led an incredibly diverse and miraculous life.

One Saturday afternoon we visited him at the VA Hospital and he asked us if we could come by and get him one day and take him down to the Naples area to walk around the old Seneca Indian burial grounds. We told him we would come get him on Columbus Day, since that would be a quiet Monday and Dad could take the day off to be with us. The entire day was wonderful, as we drove all over Naples and spent time walking through the woods and around Grimes Glen with Bob.

After dinner, just before we were ready to take Bob back to his room, he got out some x-rays he had brought with him to show us his medical condition. He explained that in a short matter of time, he would die of two blood clots leading to his heart if God did not heal him. He had several x-rays that showed how rapidly the clots were traveling. The doctors had told him to call his family and prepare to die. There was nothing they could do for him.

As I sat across the couch from him in my Dad's old chair, listening to the details of his fatal medical condition, my heart literally ached. Although we had only known Bob a short time, both Dad and I had grown very fond of him. He was a wonderfully unique and talkative man, full of life in every way. He had been so calm in the face of death that we were totally unaware of the killer clots that laid in wait to take his life.

I looked over at Dad and could tell he was as affected by Bob's story as I was. "Bob, before my Dad takes you back to the VA tonight, let's take hands and the three of us will agree, with Jesus in the midst of us, He can do a mighty miracle and heal your body. Would you like to pray together, Bob?" He nodded his old, white head and bowed to pray. The three of us took hands and my Dad and I took authority over the enemy that was trying to steal his life from him. The prayer and deliverance time was intense. It was at least an hour later when we felt the release to stop praying and began to praise God for His goodness.

In our spirits, we had felt God move and knew that a mighty miracle had taken place in my parents' living room that night. Bob was wet with perspiration. In all of the prayer sessions I had ever been in, I had never seen anyone sweat the way he did during that hour of prayer and deliverance.

At the next Full Gospel Businessman's meeting, Bob stood at the microphone beaming. He had his new set of x-rays and gave an awesome testimony of how God had healed his body of his blood clots. I remember thinking, "God, why do we ever doubt You?" Bob radiated as he told of God's amazing power and faithfulness.

Several years later, Dad told me Bob died of old age and natural causes. A true witness for Christ, he had spent the remainder of his years sharing God's faithfulness from his room in the VA Hospital in Bath, NY, to all who would listen.

A short time after our prayer session with Bob, a friend from church pulled me aside and asked me in private if I would please pray for her daughter, who had been unable to have children. "Of course I will, Betty. I homeschool my kids, so I am usually home during the day. Why don't you bring your daughter by tomorrow after lunch, around 1:30 or 2:00. Will that work for you?"

"Oh, Vicki," Betty responded, obviously excited at the prospect of prayer for her daughter. "That would be wonderful. I really do appreciate it."

The next day, Betty and her daughter appeared at my door, full of faith. I had never met her daughter before. She was young and beautiful. She and her husband had tried to conceive for years without success. The frustration in her voice was obvious as she related the painful details of her ongoing doctor's appointments and tests.

"Listen," I said emphatically, "I have personally witnessed fertility miracles. I know Jesus wants to heal your womb." I told her about a staff pastor's wife at Church on the Rock who was unable to have children and how the Holy Spirit spoke to my spirit to lay hands on her womb for healing. Within the month, the couple conceived.

"God is no respecter of persons. What He did for them, He can do for you. Do you believe that God is, and that He is a rewarder of those who diligently seek Him?"

"Oh yes, I believe that God can do anything," she exclaimed emphatically. "I have been a believer for years."

"Well, that is great. I know your mom believes God can heal you or she would not have brought you here today for prayer. Let's just go to the Lord in prayer right now and ask Him to open up your womb."

As I laid my hands on her womb and thanked the Lord for His healing virtue, I believed with all of my being she would be healed. I assured her, as she and her mom left that day, she would soon become pregnant. Before the month was out, Betty ran up to me as I walked through the church doors.

"Vicki. Wonderful news. My daughter is pregnant!" I just beamed at her. "Isn't the Lord just so good, Betty? We serve an awesome God."

Unfortunately, not everyone was as ecstatic as we were about the miracle. The next morning, I received a phone call from a voice I did not recognize. "Is this Vicki Garza, the Goddess of Fertility?" I felt like I was going to be sick to my stomach. I had no idea who this was, but the mockery in his voice literally turned my stomach.

"Who is this?" I asked.

"This is your pastor, Vicki. We need to talk."

When I put down the phone, my entire body was shaking inside. I thought about the man who had just called himself "my pastor." He was the only pastor I had ever had that was not my pastor at all. He was a layman who had appointed himself to preach when the church was first formed just over a year earlier, shortly after my Dad and I had returned from England.

The first time I met him was on Father's Day, 1986, when I had been asked to share at the church. It had been an exhilarating experience for me to be able to preach in my Dad's church on Father's Day. I was still basking in the joy of the moment when a man came up to me and introduced himself as the assistant pastor. As he was walking toward me, the Holy Spirit spoke to my spirit and told me that the man had a spirit of perversion and homosexuality. Because the church was young and there was no paid staff, this man had been allowed to assume a position of leadership in the church.

On the way home, I rode alone with my Dad. It was the perfect time to approach the subject. "Dad, I wanted to talk to you about something. I know the church is young and cannot afford to pay the leadership yet, but I think it is important that each person in leadership is placed there by God."

Dad glanced over at me as he was driving. I could tell that he was feeling defensive, but I continued. "As the assistant pastor was walking toward me this morning to introduce himself, the Lord told me that he has a spirit of perversion and homosexuality. I think He told me so I could tell you. You are in a position to do something about it."

Dad spoke slowly and with absolute confidence. "Vicki, I know this man. He has been living with the pastor and his family ever since he came to town. He is a man of God. God sent him to us. You are mistaken."

"Dad, I am positive that God spoke to me today. For the sake of the congregation, please pray about it and share it with the pastor." Now Dad was mad.

"I am not sharing it with anybody and I do not need to pray about it. You are dead wrong, Vic. Dead wrong." We rode home in awkward silence.

It had only taken about six months for the Lord to expose this man for what he was. Before he slipped out of the pastor's house in the middle of the night, this man's 1-900 phone bills had mounted to nearly $1,000. I was not sure if my Dad had shared the revelation the Lord had shown me about the assistant pastor with the pastor or not. For whatever reason, it was evident the pastor was not happy to have me in the area. And now that Betty's daughter had conceived, he was especially unhappy with me.

The Holy Spirit within me was grieved. I knew I had no other recourse but to peacefully leave the church. Without a word to anyone about it, Paco and I decided to start attending a small Bible church in Naples. There were four families in the church, including our family and the pastor's family.

After a few Sundays, I felt it was important to be honest with the pastor about the way Paco and I believed. I invited him to our home one night, mainly to put him at ease. I wanted him to know that, although we were spirit-filled Evangelical Christians, we would not impose our beliefs on his family or anyone else at the church. We knew they did not believe exactly the way we did. That was fine with us. It was refreshing to be under a pastor that was sold out to the Word of God and applied it in his own life and in the life of his family.

"Joel," I ventured, "the reason we invited you here tonight is to let you know that although we believe strongly the gifts of the Spirit are for today, and will continue to practice the gifts of the Spirit in our own home, we will respect the beliefs of your church for as long as we attend there. We won't testify publicly or even privately of the miracles we have seen God perform in our lives." I hesitated, before I continued, to see if I could get a gauge of how he was receiving my message. Uncharacteristically quiet, Joel sat across the table from me with his hands folded. When he did speak, he could not conceal his obvious contempt for the segment of Christianity that believed as we did.

"I do not believe the gifts of the spirit are for today, Vicki. If I believed the way you do, I would be in every hospital ward in Rochester, laying my hands on the sick so they could all go home!"

I had spent much time in prayer before the meeting and was not feeling the least bit defensive at his response. Knowing his theological background, I knew he most likely would not understand where we were coming from. I just wanted him to know that we would never cause any theological waves in his church. He had a right to the way he believed and it was his church. If we wanted to attend it, knowing how his beliefs differed from ours, then the burden rested on us to comply to the church's teachings, not the other way around.

By the time he left that night, we had reached an understanding. Now that I look back on it, I think I was growing tired of swimming against the flow. I just wanted to sit under a learned Bible teacher and be fed the Word of God. Subconsciously, I may have felt the body ministry I had been flowing in since the baby died was too controversial. At least for the time being, I would abstain from moving in the gifts of the spirit and try to live a more typical Christian life.

We settled into our new church just as the holidays were approaching. The pastor and his wife and six girls had come from the Amish country, where women had to wear long hair, no make-up and were banned from wearing pants. It was as different from Church on the Rock in Texas as you could get. Somehow, it was spiritually nurturing to me to just sit back and listen to the Word of God. Those holidays were some of the most memorable times we have ever spent as a family, as our kids learned how to have fun in the snow, sledding with toboggans for hours at a time.

Unfortunately, our time in that small, storefront Bible church was cut short. In February 1988, when the Jimmy Swaggart scandal broke, Joel could no longer allow our presence in his church. He found our theology offensive. After church on Sunday, we were asked to leave the church. The following evening, he and his deacon (the father of one of the other four families in the church) came to our home and asked for the church hymnal we had borrowed. It was important to Joel and to his deacon that nothing from their church remain in our possession.

Although it hurt to be excommunicated, we were not surprised, and refused to take it personally. We had known, going into the situation, that we had more respect for his beliefs than he had for ours. It was just one more Christian experience that helped us to **take our**

eyes off of man and keep them firmly planted on the Lord. The Bible says that our high priest, Jesus, is not unaware of our needs. He Himself was tempted in all ways and overcame, so that we could overcome.

In the spring, I decided to take the children to Mexico for a month to homeschool them at Paco's parents' house. It was a wonderful way to spend a warm spring after a long, cold winter. The evening of my return, after a month of not being together, Paco and I were anxious to be together as husband and wife. Knowing I had just finished my menstrual cycle, I assured him that we did not need to use any form of protection.

Within the month, I knew I had been wrong. Much to our shock, I was pregnant. My friend, Rose, had been right when she predicted I would have more children. Remembering her vision helped me to accept my unplanned pregnancy and thank God that He knew the end from the beginning. Although I had not planned to have another child, God had planned this new life from the foundation of the world. I took comfort and found strength in that fact.

By late fall, Paco accepted a new job at a fast-growing business-to-business agency in downtown Rochester. The 33 percent pay increase was an absolute Godsend, as we were finding it very difficult to make ends meet on his meager salary. With a fourth child coming, it would be impossible to make ends meet on $36,000 a year. Now that we would be making more money, we could afford to lease a home in the city so Paco would not have to commute 60 miles a day to and from work.

> *"Is anyone among you afflicted (ill-treated, suffer-ing evil)? He should pray. Is anyone glad at heart? He should sing praise [to God]. Is anyone among you sick? He should call in the church elders (the spiritual guides). And they should pray over Him, anointing him with oil in the Lord's name. And the prayer [that is] of faith will save him who is sick, and the Lord will restore him; and if he has commit-ted sins, he will be forgiven. Confess to one another therefore your faults (your slips, your false steps,*

your offenses, your sins) and pray [also] for one another, that you may be restored [to a spiritual tone of mind and heart]. The earnest, (heartfelt) continued prayer of a righteous man makes tremendous power available [dynamic in its working]."

James 5:13-16

CHAPTER 11

Rochester Battles And Blessings

I knew, once the baby was born, we would have to put the children back into public schools. I had made a list of what we needed in a home and set it before the Lord in prayer. My sister Luanne and I had been faithful to pray for an hour or more a day for over a year, so I had confidence the Lord would order our steps as we made our move to the city.

Finally, we found the perfect house in the best school district in Rochester. It was in a beautiful, mature neighborhood and had an in-ground pool. It definitely exceeded even my expectations of what God had in mind for our new home. After meeting with the realtor, the kids and I sat out in the driveway in our car.

"Okay, kids. Do you believe that this is the home that God has hand-picked for us to live in?"

"Yes, Mommy! We love it. Let's get it."

The only problem with the house was the price. It was 40 percent more than we had budgeted for our monthly rent. No wonder it was so much nicer than anything else we had seen.

"If God wants us to have this house, He will have to perform a miracle and move on the owners' hearts to lower the price. Will you all agree with me in prayer and ask the Lord to do that for us? Let's all extend our hands toward the house and pray."

My five-, seven- and nine-year old children all straightened their little arms out and prayed with me for a miracle. As we drove away that day, I had perfect peace that God was going to move on the hearts of the owners to reduce the price. By December 1st, we were living in the nicest home we had ever lived in. Paco had a dream job as senior creative director over a staff of six other artists and our children were enrolled in the most acclaimed public school in the city.

Our new life was so much greater than anything I had ever imagined. Little did we know, it was just the beginning of the many blessings God was to perform in our lives.

"Honey, I heard there is an inner-city church that has a wonderful cantata during the Christmas Holidays. Do you want to go?"

"Sure, Vic. I will try anything once."

As we hurried around getting the children ready for church, I could feel the excitement building in my spirit. It had been a year and a half since we had driven away from Dallas and our beloved Church on the Rock.

"Oh Lord," I prayed. "Please show us if Bethel is the church you have picked for us. You know how Paco and I long to find a true church family for ourselves and our children."

On the way home from the cantata that night, our spirits were riding high. Even though there was no sermon, we had both felt such a kindred spirit with the members of the congregation. We just knew we were home.

A few weeks before John was born in February, we were in the balcony of the church preparing to leave. The service had just ended, when one of the ushers approached us.

"I have seen your family here for a few times now," he said as he introduced himself. "I was wondering if you would like me to take you down to the altar to meet Pastor Domina." I graciously thanked him, but in my spirit, I did not feel the time was right.

"I really appreciate your kind offer. However, I think we will wait and let the Holy Spirit introduce us to the pastor." I just knew in my spirit the Lord wanted to introduce us to the Dominas in His own special way in His time.

True to His Word, the Lord created a divinely appointed time for us to meet the pastor and his wife later on that spring. We all felt an instant rapport in the Lord. By July, we had become close friends with the Domina family, and together we shared personal time.

The Dominas were an inspiration to our lives at a time when we were feeling lost and disconnected in a new environment. God really used them to bring healing to our hearts. Not since Pastor Larry and his wife had we felt such a spiritual connection with a pastor and his wife.

Right after John's birth, Paco told me that he wanted to hurry and get a vasectomy before I could get pregnant again. I instantly felt a red flag go up in my spirit.

"Honey, what if God wants us to have more children? Who are we to stop the Lord from performing His perfect will in our lives if He has another child in store for us?" Paco was unyielding.

"Vic," he said with frustration, "haven't you figured out yet that kids are expensive? We cannot afford to have any more children. God knows our financial condition. He understands. I am making an appointment to get a vasectomy and that is that."

Whoa. He obviously felt very strongly about this. It reminded me of his plans to get a vasectomy after Paquito was born. I shuddered to think how different our lives would have been if we could not have had David and John. I had learned over the years, when my own arguments did not work with Paco, to turn the situation over to the Lord.

"The ball is in your court, Lord. You know my hands are tied. If You have another child for us, You will have to make a way for his conception."

Paco was so paranoid. He seemed to be avoiding me. The few times we were intimate, he would use double protection, just to be sure. He was bound and determined to stop at four children.

Friday afternoon, Paco strolled in from work with a smile on his face. "Well," he said smugly, "I have a vasectomy appointment with Dr. Stop on Tuesday. You have to come with me to my first appointment."

My heart sunk. I really did not want to go through with it. "You may have to take one of the girls from the office with you to pose as your wife," I teased. Then in a more serious tone, I added, "Honey, I cannot honestly tell the doctor I am in agreement with you to get a vasectomy when I am not." He stiffened and I could tell he was growing impatient.

"Vicki, this is really important to me. Would you please just do this for me?"

"I don't know, Paco. I will go on Tuesday, but I cannot promise you anything."

Sunday night the phone rang. It was my friend Kathy from Daytona Beach. She and I had met our senior year in high school in New York City. Although we had been very close for several years through college, we had lost touch with one another in 1977. I had written a note to her in1986 and sent it to her childhood home. It was the only address I had for her. Fortunately, her parents forwarded the letter to her. Ever since, she and I had been communicating by phone calls and letters.

"Kathy, what a pleasant surprise!"

"Vicki," she said. "I just had a brainstorm. I am visiting an old friend in New York City and just realized there is absolutely nothing to stop me from coming to visit you. We haven't seen each other in twelve years! I know you just had a baby, but do you think you are up to having company come by for a few days?"

"Don't be silly, Kath. I would love to see you. When are you coming?"

"I just called the airline and changed my reservations. I can fly in Tuesday morning and stay until Friday. Does that work for you guys?"

"Of course it does. I'm anxious to see you again, Kathy. Thanks for calling."

When I hung up, I looked at Paco.

"Honey, the vasectomy appointment with Dr. Stop will have to wait. I haven't seen Kathy in twelve years. I am sure not going to abandon her to go to a doctor's appointment that can easily be rescheduled for another time. We never have company."

Paco was surprisingly understanding of the situation. "Okay. I will call and reschedule for next week. A week shouldn't make a difference."

"Thanks, sweetie. I love you so much," I said as I threw my

arms around his neck. At that moment, I felt such a surge of gratitude for him. The Lord really knew what He was doing when He brought us together.

Much to Paco's chagrin, a week did make a difference. The following week, Paco and I sat growing more and more impatient as we waited for the nurse to call us in to see Dr. Stop. Finally, Paco went to the nurse's station and pulled the glass window back. We had been waiting for nearly an hour.

"Oh, I am so sorry, Mr. Garza. Didn't anyone tell you? The doctor was called away a short while ago on a personal emergency. He will not be able to see you today."

Paco was obviously upset. "When can we see the doctor?"

"Well, let me see," the nurse said as she ran her finger down his appointment schedule. "He is very busy the next few weeks. I can set up an appointment for two weeks from now."

I just smiled to myself, hoping the Lord was up to something. By the time Paco and I had met with Dr. Stop and scheduled his surgery, it was already June. Although he was in terrible pain, Paco was pleased with the fact that he had finally taken care of his ability to father children. He decided to call his parents and tell them the good news.

"Dad, I just wanted to let you know we are all done having children. I had my surgery today. I thought you would like to know Vicki and I are stopping at four." After he hung up, he looked at me. A look of concern crossed his face as he said, "Hey, Vic, aren't you supposed to be getting your period sometime soon?"

"Don't worry," I answered. "I am sure it will come." He had been so cautious, I honestly did not see how God was going to override Paco's decision and give us a child. "I guess I was wrong, Lord," I thought. "I was so positive You had one more son for us."

Nine days later, my kids and I were at the park with my sister, Marcia, and her family. The children were playing in the water and she and I sat talking at the picnic table. Rather casually, I mentioned that I was nine days late for my period.

Marcia got excited. "Vicki, I will bet you anything that you are pregnant!"

"Yeah, right," I said sarcastically. "That would take a miracle.

Paco had been staying clear of me until he had his vasectomy."

Marcia just sat there, unmoved by my statement. "Vicki, I am telling you, you are pregnant. I just know you are."

I did not even feel a stirring in my spirit. I had given up all hope. "I am not, Marcia. I can guarantee you, I am not."

"Well," she said slowly. "Why don't we just go over to the Crisis Pregnancy Center and get you tested? We don't have anything better to do today."

"Marcia, if that will make you feel better, I will go. But I will tell you right now, I am not pregnant."

"Oh come on, Vic. It will be fun. My friend Dee is in charge of the center. She will be thrilled just to see you and your kids again." A few minutes later, I sat incredulous, staring at the pink plus sign on the table in front of me. I was dumbfounded. "How did You do that, Lord?" I mused. "Paco was so careful not to get me pregnant before he had his vasectomy."

That night, Paco picked up the phone to call his father. "Dad, you are not going to believe this. Vicki just found out today that she is pregnant. I guess we weren't done after all!" When he hung up the phone, I put my hand over his.

"Honey, please be happy. You know you did everything in your power to stop me from getting pregnant. The Lord just overrode you, that is all. He knew He had another child planned for us." Daniel Jordan was born the following February, just one year after Kathy had visited our home in Rochester.

Our years in Rochester were good years. Although there was never quite enough money to go around with seven mouths to feed, somehow we made it. Our church family was wonderful and we had made many close friends. The days of Church on the Rock and Dallas seemed to fade more and more into the distance. Once again, I felt mentally, physically and spiritually fit.

That same year, in the fall of 1990, we sent Elisa to Mexico to spend the year with her aunt and uncle and cousins to attend school there. At the end of 5th grade, when we had finished our home school for the year, I had her tested. She had tested out exceptionally high in all of her subjects, so we knew she could afford to take it easy her 6th grade year.

Our Mexican nephew, Mario, came to live with us in Rochester and attend school there. I decided to put my children into St. John's school with Mario, since I could no longer homeschool them with two children under the age of two. When school started that fall, I committed myself to two hours of prayer daily while the boys took their morning naps.

A lot happened that Fall. My dear friend and intercessory prayer partner, Rose, flew up from Dallas the last week of September to spend some time with me. When she arrived, she suggested we fast and pray for three days and ask God for a miraculous break in our lives and finances.

She knew how tight things had been for us. In confidence, I had mentioned that I did not know how we were ever going to get out of debt, let alone get ahead financially. At the ages of 36 and 34, we still did not have a savings account or any investments worth mentioning. Other than our rental home in Dallas, which was still mortgaged, and the home we had lived in since 1984, which had a negatively amortized mortgage, we really did not own much. Both of our cars were over seven years old. At least we did own them.

After three days of fasting and praying, we broke our fast with a dinner meal. After dinner, Paco played worship songs on the piano as we all sang. It was a wonderful evening, warm with Christian fellowship.

After we put the children in bed for the night, Paco, Rose and I gathered in the living room to talk. "Rose," I said. "I don't think I told you that this is always a difficult date for us. Eight years ago today was the day Paquito died. I just wanted you to know that having you here, praying with us, has made it easier."

Rose was evidently touched and reached out to take my hand and Paco's hand in hers. "You two are very special to me. Although I did not know you yet, I am sure you glorified God through your grief."

Paco's reaction was immediate. "You don't know, Rose. You don't know. You cannot even imagine how hard it was for me to have all of these fanatical Christians picking up my son's body from his coffin, commanding him to come to life days after he had died. It killed me to have my parents watch, as their own hearts were breaking with grief over our son's death. It was a horrible thing. It makes me very angry just to think about it."

I had not realized that Paco was still harboring bitterness and anger over the scene in the funeral parlor. I was thrilled to have Christian friends who were willing to believe with me for such a mighty miracle. To hear Paco's version of that day, it was more like a bizarre circus. I looked at him sadly. His perspective was so different from my own.

"Paco has not cried since a few weeks after the baby died, Rose. I have cried on and off many times over the years. But Paco has not cried in over eight years. He refuses to talk about it or think about it. It has really been hard."

"Oh, Paco," Rose said with compassion. "That whole episode had to have been so horrible for you." As Rose reached over and put her arm around Paco, he hung his head sadly. Then he started to weep. He wept slowly at first, then faster and louder until he was crying uncontrollably. Tears began to stream down both Rose and my cheeks as we watched with compassion. Paco had completely lost himself in his grief.

"Paco," Rose continued. "You have to give your grief, your anger, your bitterness and your unforgiveness to God. Can you do that right now?" Paco nodded as he continued to cry, his face distorted with pain.

"Yes," he said. "Yes, Lord, I release my anger and my grief, my bitterness and unforgiveness. I forgive each one of those people for making my son's death into a circus and for shaming me in front of my parents. I forgive them, Lord." We all just sat quietly for a while, as Paco pulled himself together.

I moved over to sit next to Paco, and was rubbing my hand on his knee, trying to give him some emotional support. Rose knelt down before us and pulled out her small bottle of anointing oil.

"I am going to pray for you two, that the Lord will give you both a fresh sense of His power and His presence in your lives." Then she started to pray in the spirit, under her breath at first. Gradually, her voice steadily grew louder until she was speaking over us loudly in tongues. Her hand was waving rhythmically over our foreheads, just as the prophetess had the night I received my prophecy over David.

"Thus saith the Lord," she said with authority. "Paco and Vicki, I have brought you together for a purpose...you will have an advertising agency that will bring glory and honor to My name. I have seen your hearts and know your innermost desires. I will use the foolish things of the world to confound the wise. Promotion comes from Me, saith the Lord. Everyone who looks upon you will marvel at what I have done in your lives. Do not doubt Me in this. Only believe."

When she had finished praying, I opened my eyes and exclaimed, "But Rose, I don't want to have an advertising agency. I just want to stay home with my kids and be a stay-at-home mom. I like the way my life is right now. I don't want to change anything."

"Vicki," Rose said forcefully. "You do not understand. I am not the message-maker. I am just the messenger. You will have to talk to the Lord about what He has planned for you."

A foreboding feeling came over me as I sat back on the couch, trying to take in everything the Lord had just spoken to us. "What is up with this, Lord? I thought for sure You brought us to Rochester. You are the one who gave Paco favor with the people here in Rochester and gave our family favor in our church. You know I love just being a mom and staying home with my kids."

Before long, God would reveal His perfect will to us regarding our future. But first, He had another battle for me to fight.

One day in early October, the kids came running in after school. Jessica, just nine, was especially animated as she told me about how their bus had been decorated for Halloween. "You should see it, Mommy. It has witches and a bloody Frankenstein and skeletons all over it. Yuck!" Jessica exclaimed, making a face. "It is really scary."

The next morning, when I walked the children to the bus stop, I waited for the bus to come. Sure enough, the Halloween images on the bus were larger than life. They were all taped on the bottom half of the windows, so the children could not even see out. I watched, horrified, as David ran onto the bus and looked for a seat. Since my children were the last stop before the bus drove to the school, his choices were limited. There was only one empty seat. It had a very realistic wicked witch with ugly bumps all over her nose and an evil grin on her ghoulish, green face.

"Mary," I said to the bus driver, as I boarded the bus with my children, "our kids do not celebrate Halloween. These images are really scaring them. Would you mind removing them?"

Mary responded in a tone full of disgust, "I just decorated this bus yesterday and it will stay decorated this way until the day after Halloween. I decorate my bus this way every year." I glanced back at my children and Mario, who were all surrounded by the wicked Halloween images on every side.

As I left the bus, I decided to bring a camera with me in the morning. In the meantime, I made a phone call to the principal and the foreman of the bus garage. No matter whom I called, I got the same answer. "Mary has a right to decorate her bus the way she wants to. It is her bus."

The next morning, I boarded the bus again, this time with my camera. I got a close up photo of the witch, so I could show Paco and others whom I knew would be concerned. During my morning prayer time, I beseeched the Lord for an answer to the dilemma. "Lord, you know my children have never been de-sensitized to evil images. I have raised them in Your Word, so they have not been exposed to very much television or other worldly ways. I really need your help here, Lord."

The following weekend, I was telling my sister Marcia about how traumatizing it was to my children to be forced to sit next to wicked images on the school bus. Not a day went by that they did not complain of nightmares and irrepressible bad thoughts.

Marcia heard me out, then asked, "Vicki, do any of the children display any physical evidence or manifestations of being traumatized?"

"I took David to the doctor this week because he has hives all over his body. I didn't even connect the hives with his being traumatized."

"There is your answer," Marcia said. "Contact the school authorities and let them know that your son has been physically affected by the images. After all, Vic, he is only seven. If you don't defend him, who will?"

The following Monday, I contacted everyone I thought could help me at the school, mentioning the physical manifestations David had experienced. They agreed to hold a special board meeting that night on the subject. After the meeting, I got a call. Regardless of the trauma to our son, the decision to leave the decorations up on the bus stood. Mary had a right to decorate her bus the way she wanted.

The next morning, as I prayed and pled my case before the Lord, I felt as though I was David against Goliath. "What do I do now, Lord? Every way I turn, I am being shut down. Please show me that one smooth stone, the one thing that will bring this giant down."

The Holy Spirit spoke to me and told me to call the Rochester Democrat and Chronicle. I immediately did as He said. My voice was unwavering as I spoke with the reporter on the other end of the phone. My heart sunk, as he listened, emotionally unmoved. He thanked me for calling and said he would get back with me if the paper chose to do a story. It seemed to be a condescending way of saying "Thanks, but no thanks."

As I hung up, I wondered if I had really heard from the Lord. A few minutes later, my phone rang. It was the reporter. "Mrs. Garza? I just spoke to my editor. We would like to do a front-page article on your story tonight. Did you say you have a photograph of that witch? Could I send a courier over to your house right now to pick it up? Also, do you have some time to answer a few questions for me?"

When I put down the phone, I was so happy I could have burst. The Lord had indeed given me that one smooth stone. That night, I stopped by our local gas station to get gas and a paper. As I ran inside to pay, a big yellow sign hanging from the newspaper rack stopped me dead in my tracks. It read: "EAST ROCHESTER HALLOWEEN CONTROVERSY."

"Wow, Lord," I thought. "When you do something, you do it right!"

I bought a paper and left, reading it as I walked back to the car. Sure enough, there was the picture of the witch. Next to the photo was a half page article detailing what all I had been through in an effort to get the images removed from the bus.

Not surprisingly, the next morning I got a call from the principal of St. Johns' school. The decorations had been removed from the bus.

After the phone call, I stood still and meditated on the goodness of God. "Lord, there is nothing impossible with You." I vowed to always ask Him first and involve Him in my deepest needs and concerns. I was reminded of the scripture, **"The Lord will perfect those things that concern me."**

One day in mid-December, I was watching *The 700 Club* as I waited for the kids to come home from school. Pat Robertson was interviewing Charles Givens, a man who had written several books about strategies to save money and get out of debt. For some reason, I was so stirred by what this man had to say, I knew I had to get his books. When the kids got home from school, I packed everyone into the car and drove straight to the store to buy two of his books.

In the next two days, I had read them both and made several pages of notes. The hope I felt after reading his books was inde-scribable. For the first time in a long time, I felt supercharged and energized, armed with a plan of action for getting out of debt and saving money.

I stayed up late, praying over the notes I had taken, waiting to hear from the Lord. It was almost midnight and Paco was nearly asleep. "Honey." I prodded him with my elbow. "Are you awake?" I whispered.

Paco turned toward me and murmured sleepily, "What is it honey? I was asleep."

"Do you know how I was telling you that Charles Givens recommends you start a freelance business from your home for tax purposes and additional income? I was sitting here thinking of names for your graphic design and illustration business. What do you think of the name 'The Garza Creative Group'?"

"I like it," he said. "Can I go to sleep now?"

I was too excited to sleep. "Lord," I prayed. "What are you about to do in our lives?" I knew intuitively that something big was about to happen. I had no idea how big. Our lives were about to take a twist that would change our futures forever.

In retrospect, I am thankful the Lord only showed me a small glimpse at a time. I am not sure I could have believed Him for the enormity of what He was about to do in our lives.

New Year's Eve, 1990, we had a gathering of Christian friends come over to ring in the New Year. As midnight approached, I asked everybody to pull his or her chair into a circle in the living room. Giving them a few minutes to consult with the Lord and with each other, every couple was asked to give one New Year Resolution. It had to be something they felt strongly enough about to keep. As everybody shared his or her dreams that night, it was finally time for Paco and me to share ours.

"We want to start a freelance computer-based graphic design business from our home this year," Paco stated with confidence. "We have named our business 'The Garza Creative Group.' We are praying the Lord will supply the finances and the clients to make our dream a reality."

Everyone around the room nodded their head with approval. "We have always wanted to do something together," I piped in. "We feel this is a joint dream the Lord has given us. We believe God wants to use our compound talents for His glory."

They were just dreams, after all, but they felt so real as we shared them with one another that night.

> *"For I know the thoughts and plans I have for you, says the Lord, thoughts and plans for welfare and peace and not for evil, to give you hope in your final outcome. Then you will call upon Me, and you will come and pray to Me, and I will hear and heed you. Then you will seek Me, inquire for, and require Me [as a vital necessity] and find Me when you search for Me with all your heart. I will be found by you, says the Lord, I will release you from captivity and gather you from all the nations and all the places to which I have driven you, says the Lord, and I will bring you back to the place from which I caused you to be carried captive."*
>
> *Jeremiah 29:11-14*

CHAPTER 12

An Ad Agency Is Birthed

❧

New Year's Day, Paco and I were reflecting on the previous evening. The first New Year's party we had ever hosted had been a huge success. "That was fun, honey. We should have people over to our house more often," I said, full of enthusiasm.

Paco was noticeably distracted. "Vicki," Paco said. I could tell by the stilted way he said my name he was thinking about something that was difficult for him to talk about. "I have to tell you something."

"What is it, sweetheart?" I held my breath as I awaited his answer. It seemed strange for Paco to be so serious.

"I have been praying a lot lately. I am pretty sure the Lord has spoken something to me."

I sat straight up in my chair. I sensed whatever he was about to say was very important.

"Tell me, Paco. What did the Lord tell you?"

"The Lord told me He is going to move us back to Dallas this year. I think He is going to do it very soon."

I sat silent for a moment, groping for my own words. This news was coming to me from left field. The Lord had not indicated this to me in any way. Finally, after a time of awkward silence, I voiced my doubt out loud. I tried to choose my words carefully. "Are you sure you are not just wishing you were back in Dallas and what you thought was God's voice was actually just your own wishful thinking?"

Paco was not budging.

"You know how you are always telling me God told you something and it is hard for me to believe you because He didn't tell me? Now you know how *I* feel."

It was true. Paco seldom understood when God spoke to me. However, to his credit, he always allowed me to move forward if I was convinced God had spoken. I had often thought his blind obedience would be credited to him for righteousness. When Thomas had demanded a sign, Jesus said, "Blessed are those who have not seen and yet believe."

So now it was my turn to be in the dark and obey in blind faith. I took a deep breath and answered him, "You are right, honey. Who am I to say? If God wants to take us back to Dallas this year, I am up for it. It will take a miracle, to be sure. You know as well as I do we have never been able set aside money for emergency use or savings. Only God knows how much a move like that will cost and where the money will come from." Paco agreed. Although he didn't know where the money was going to come from, he was unwavering in his faith. God had spoken a word to his spirit, and he knew it.

A few days later, completely confident he had truly heard from God, Paco took a step of faith and called his father. "Dad, I wanted to tell you that Vicki and I are planning on moving our family back to Dallas this year. We are going to start looking for work in Dallas right away." He was nodding his head as he listened closely to his dad's wise advice. "Don't worry, Dad. I won't do anything foolish, I promise. I would never leave a good paying job in New York to move to Dallas without a job."

After he hung up, he just looked at me quietly for a minute. His eyes searched mine as if he was looking for reassurance. "I sure hope I heard from God, Vic. I'm going to look like a real fool if I am wrong."

"Listen to me, Paco," I said with strong conviction. "I have complete faith you did hear from God. Now we just have to proceed, believing that God will finish what He started in us. James 2:17 says that faith without works is dead. Let's put action to our faith and start to put together plans for your resume and portfolio. I have such a witness in my spirit right now. I have a feeling this move is going to change our lives in a major way."

That was January 3,1991. In a step of faith, Paco contacted a photographer friend to see if he would take a couple of shots of him to use on a promotional piece Paco had designed for himself. The flyer he designed was a takeoff of <u>Adweek</u>, a popular publication in our industry. The masthead read <u>Adleak</u>. The feature story on the front cover was Paco, standing confidently with his arms crossed. The subhead read, "Garza up for Grabs." The rest of the story was an overview of his career and highlighted his clients and award-winning campaigns with Kodak, Xerox and Bausch and Lomb.

Within hours, I had written the copy for the piece on the first pass. Monday morning, Paco sent the copy along with his resume to the typesetter to set the type. In a few short days, we had thrown the flyer together with little effort. The process flowed so naturally, we were sure the Lord had His hand in it. It felt as though He had released a special anointing upon us.

That same Monday morning, just three days from the evening Paco had called his dad, I laid my two sons down for naps and went to the couch to pray. I had been praying every morning for one to two hours while the babies slept. As I knelt by my couch to pray, I sensed the Lord was going to do a new thing that morning. Nearly an hour of fervent, heartfelt prayer had passed, when I began to thank the Lord for meeting our needs, even before we knew we had a need. I will never forget the alarm I felt in my spirit as the Holy Spirit spoke to my spirit. Almost instantly, the Lord spoke to me so clearly it seemed as though he was next to me: "Do not forget those words, Vicki."

I immediately stopped praying. A deep chill had just moved from my neck, down my spine to my tailbone. Suddenly, I had the most foreboding feeling. "Lord Jesus," I whispered with choked emotion. "What is about to happen? Please tell me what is going on." There was a chilling feeling moving over me that I just could not shake. I tried to pray past it, but it was too late. I was totally spooked. Finally, I decided it was no use to remain in prayer. My spirit was churning with a mixture of fear and dread. Unable to keep my mind off of the Holy Spirit's ominous warning, I decided to go upstairs to take a shower to try to get warm.

In the hot shower, I continued praying, this time in the spirit. As I prayed feverishly, I tried not to panic. I knew deep in my innermost spirit that something life changing was about to happen. Remembering the foreboding feeling I had felt just before the baby died, I tried to keep my mind from flashing back. In a futile effort to remove the chill that had settled deep in my bones, I turned the faucet to the hottest setting. No matter how hard I had tried to warm up, the bitter cold would not leave me. My body shook as I stepped out of the shower and hit the cold air. I grabbed a towel from the counter and was drying off, when the Holy Spirit spoke again. Once again, the instructions were so clear it was as though He was standing next to me.

"Vicki, I want you to put on some nice clothes, make up your face and wait at the kitchen table for Paco. He is coming home in a few minutes."

The feeling of doom I felt at this new directive was all encompassing. I felt as though my heart had just fallen to my knees. I had a strong urge to vomit, I was feeling so nervous and nauseous. Breathing deep, I sat down on the bed and tried to pull myself together.

"Lord, this must be important. I don't ever remember Paco coming home in the middle of the day."

As I carefully chose my clothes and put on my makeup, my body was still shaking. I had a horrible premonition that the Lord was preparing me once again for a very difficult walk of faith.

As I waited at the kitchen table for Paco to come home, I had time to reflect on the details of the morning. When the Lord told me to remember those words – that He knew our need even before we knew we had a need – I wondered what He could possibly take us through that we had not already been through. Sometimes, we felt like Paul when he described all of the conditions he had suffered for the Lord. We had known abject poverty, we had experienced persecution from friends and family that did not understand our walk of faith, and we had buried our baby son. As I sat reminiscing about all we had been through in our young lives, tears began to well up in my eyes. My soul was troubled. What else did God have in store for us? I had shivers just thinking about it. "Oh, Jesus," I prayed silently. "Please give me the strength I need to go through whatever circumstances I am about to enter. You know how human and weak I am feeling right now. In my weakness, You are made strong."

Just then, Paco walked through the door, interrupting my pensiveness. His face was ashen. He was visibly shaken. The look on his face betrayed the fear and panic he was feeling in his heart.

I was at a loss for words. Not knowing how to react, I decided it was very important to remain calm." Hi, honey," I managed to blurt out. I took a deep breath and tried to keep my voice even. "What brings you home so early?"

"Vic," Paco's voice came low and hushed. It sounded like he was going to cry any minute. His throat tightened as he struggled to speak, "I have been in Jerry's office all morning." He let out a deep sigh and cleared his throat. I could not recall ever seeing Paco so visibly shaken, other than when the baby died. I tried to stop the dread I felt flooding my own heart, as I laid my hand gently over his.

"It is okay, honey," I whispered softly. "Whatever happened, it is going to be okay."

Paco's eyes searched mine. I could tell he was hurting. Finally, he pulled himself together enough to speak.

"I just lost my job, Vic. Jerry laid me off." He breathed in deep and sat back in his chair. Laying his head back, he just stared up at the ceiling as if in disbelief. "I still cannot believe it. I did everything right. I worked hard and gave him my all. I just cannot believe that my all was not enough."

It was as though he had just struck a truth and the pain of that truth was too much to bear. In utter despair, he thrust his head into his hands and started to shake. Low moans mixed with deep sobs racked his body. Tears instantly streamed down my cheeks as I was overcome with emotion. His pain was so intense. As it ripped through his body, I could feel it engulfing my soul. I pulled him to me and held him tight.

The words the Holy Spirit had spoken to me earlier gently prodded my spirit. For the first time since Paco had walked in the door, I felt a warm peace fill my heart. It was all going to be all right. God had known all along that Paco would lose his job that day.

Once Paco had pulled himself together, I picked up his head, cupping his face in my hands. "Darling," I said softly. "The Lord spoke to me clearly this morning. He told me that He knew our needs even before we knew we had a need. None of this has taken Him by surprise. Don't you remember what you told your dad a few nights ago? You said you would never leave a good paying job in Rochester to go to Dallas without a job. This latest round of events has been ordained by the Lord. He knew you would never leave your job to return to Dallas, so He arranged for you to lose your job so you would be free to go back to Dallas. Don't you see, honey?" I said, with increasing confidence creeping into my voice. "God has a plan and this is part of it. We need to rejoice and be glad."

Paco's face reflected a newfound calmness and peace. As he wiped away his tears and sat back in his chair, I could tell he was reflecting on my words and the events of the past week. When he did speak, he was like a different man.

"You know, honey, all morning I have been so upset. I just could not believe that Jerry had the gall to hire me away from my other job in May and fire me in January. His excuse for laying me off seemed so lame. Jerry hired me to take his place as senior creative director at the agency and I did the job well. It seemed so cruel that he decided he wanted his job back so he could be more hands-on and art direct again. When he told me he was up all night wrestling with the decision, I didn't even believe him. But now I realize the Holy Spirit must have laid that decision on his heart."

"It is so obvious, honey, now that we see it," I said emphatically. "This has to be a part of God's plan for our lives. He must have great things in store for us. I have to tell you, Paco, I am relieved to finally know exactly what God was preparing me for this morning. In comparison to what could have happened, losing your job is not all that bad. If we look at the bright side, we all have our health. And we all have each other."

Ever since the baby had died, my perspective on life had totally changed. Money was just money. Debt was just debt. Problems were just problems. Compared to the loss of a human life, everything else paled in comparison.

"Yeah, you're right," Paco said. "Jerry told me it had nothing to do with my work. He said I was a great creative director. He offered to keep me on at the agency or he could pay me in full for two months of work and I could leave today."

"What did you decide to do?"

"I would definitely rather be at work than at home worrying. I told him I had a lot of jobs on my plate that needed to be finished up and I would prefer to stay on at the agency for another two months."

"I think that was wise. You are always happier when you are busy. By the way, let me tell you about *my* day. When you hear how God has been speaking to me this morning, you will be very encouraged. None of this has taken Him by surprise."

Paco and I sat at the table and laughed and cried as we compared notes on both of our mornings. It had been an eventful day, to say the least. Once Paco got over the initial shock of it all, he began to see how God could definitely work out this twist in our lives to our full advantage.

I was thankful the Lord had spoken to Paco directly about the move back to Dallas. Now that God had removed his job, he was more convinced than ever he had heard from God. His faith was unwavering. It was good to have the old Paco back.

I was filled with love and admiration for this wonderful man who had devoted his life to serving God and family. Silently, I thanked God for him. I knew most men would not be so determined to obey God's voice.

When I really meditated on how we met, it seemed as though God had searched heaven and earth to bring him to me. The chances of a foreign exchange student from Monterrey, Mexico, coming to live in my small town of sixty houses in Upstate New York, was highly improbable. When he had been given three choices of where he wanted to live in the United States, New York State was not even on his list. But the Lord in His wisdom had other plans for him. He knew how much I needed Paco to become who He wanted me to be. I hugged myself just thinking about how much the Lord loved me to give me such a wonderful life partner.

Over the next week, we both tried to figure out the logistics of the move. In our hearts, we were both very aware an uphill battle awaited us. Most pressing was the question of finances. I could not help but wonder how God was planning to pay for our cross-country move. As usual, He had everything under control.

Just over a week after we had learned of Paco's layoff, my Mom called. "Hey, Vic. I have some good news. We finally found a buyer for our business. One of our competitors is going to buy us out."

"That is great, Mom. I am really happy for you guys. I know you have been trying to work that deal out for awhile."

"Yes, we have. It has not been easy, but the wait has been worth it. The new owner will pay us a percentage up front and we will finance the rest on a fifteen-year installment loan. We close in thirty days."

"You guys have worked hard, Mom. You definitely deserve it."

"Well, you know, Vic, we have worked hard. It is nice to finally see us all reap the rewards of our hard work. You are in on this too, you know."

"Oh, I am?" I asked. "How so?"

"Don't you remember the stock that your Dad and I issued to you years ago when we incorporated? You are selling your stock as well."

"I am? How much am I selling my stock for?"

"Just the cash portion is $5,000, which you will receive at the closing in 30 days. The balance will be paid out to you over time."

"Wow, Mom, that is awesome news. Thank you so much!"

The second I hung up, I ran over to Paco. "Hey, honey, give me a high-five."

He reached up and clapped my hand with his. "What is the high-five for?"

"That, my dear, is for the $5,000 I am receiving from the sale of my parents' business in mid-February – just in time to finance our cross-country move."

Paco came around to where I was standing and gave me a big hug. "See, honey? I told you that God would work it all out. Just think, it won't be long now and we will be back in Dallas."

I thought about it for a minute. Less than a week had passed since Paco had told me that he felt God had told him He was going to move us back to Dallas. At the time, it sounded so impossible to me. I had felt like Sarah, Abraham's wife. I had actually laughed in my heart like she did when she was told she would bear a child in her old age. I distinctly remembered feeling overwhelmed by the impossibility of that idea. And here it was actually happening.

"Wow, Lord, you are something else," I thought, as I bowed my heart before Him. "Help me to never, ever doubt You."

A few weeks later, the Gulf War broke out. I was preparing to go to my weekly Bible study, when the Holy Spirit spoke to me again. "Do you remember what Pat Robertson said would happen if war breaks out?"

"Of course I do, Lord. He said the stock market would respond positively almost immediately."

"Well, what are you waiting for, Vicki? Open the Asset Management Account you learned about from Charles Givens at the banking center in the city today. Invest the money in blue chip stocks."

"Okay, Lord. This is weird. You know I don't have any money. What money am I supposed to use to invest?"

"The money your children inherited from your Grandma Ann. You have $10,000 in that account."

"But Lord, that is my children's money. I'm just supposed to invest it wisely."

"Exactly. This will be a very wise investment. Trust me. I will tell you where to invest the money."

I called my Bible study leader and told her I would be a little late, since I had an errand to run. Then I called to get directions to the banking center. My heart was beating wildly. I felt flushed and nervous, as though I was doing something illegal. Our first three children had inherited $2,500 each when Grandma Ann died. In all of the years I had overseen those accounts, it had never occurred to me to invest their money in anything risky. I had never invested in the stock market. I did not have the foggiest idea where to begin.

As I walked through the door, I tried to act calm, as though I knew what I was doing. There were symbols and numbers moving rapidly across the overhead screens. I felt so out of place. "I would like to open an Asset Management Account, please," I said in as professional a tone as I could. "I have $10,000 to open the account,"

I said, pushing the check in front of her.

"Certainly, Mrs. Garza. How would you like to invest your funds?"

"I would like to buy stock, please."

"Would you like to buy individual company stock or mutual funds?"

"I'm not sure. What is the difference?" After she had explained the difference, I decided mutual funds sounded safer.

"Which mutual funds would you like to buy, Mrs. Garza?"

This was the tough part. "Lord, are you there? Help, please!" When I didn't get an immediate answer from the Lord, I panicked. "Do you have a listing of mutual funds that I could study for a few minutes, then come back and tell you?"

She smiled warmly. "Of course, Mrs. Garza. Take all of the time you need."

I took the list and sat down in the reception area, running my index finger down the list as I read. "Okay, Lord. I am depending on you," I prayed. "Please direct my decision." As my eye traveled down the list, I saw The Founders Family of Funds. There were several funds under the listing; blue chip, international, growth fund, etc. "Pat Robertson built the Founder's Inn recently, Lord. This family of funds sounds good to me. What do You think?"

I felt good about the decision as I went back to see the broker. "I will divide the money equally between this family of funds."

"Very well, Mrs. Garza. That takes care of your business today. Have a nice day," she said as she handed me my receipts.

I walked out of the door feeling good about what I had just done. "Why didn't I think of that, Lord?" It sure was nice to have such a trustworthy financial advisor. I had a strong feeling my first mutual fund purchase would be profitable.

The end of February came before we knew it. It had been one of the craziest weeks of my life. Just a month had passed since I had made my investment. Now that it was time to go, I felt a prompting in my spirit to sell the stock and transfer the money to cash. I called the office to see how much the stock was now worth.

I hung up the phone in disbelief. "Honey," I said emphatically. "You are never going to believe how much money the kid's stocks made in one month." My mouth was hanging wide open.

"How much?" he asked, only mildly curious.

Just over $2,000.

"What?" Paco yelled. I thought he was going to fall off of the chair. "You got a $2,000 return on a $10,000 investment in 30 days? I am shocked."

I felt flushed all over. I couldn't believe it myself. I had not even called to check up on the investment. I had hardly thought about it since. I had no idea it could be so much.

"Wow, Paco. God is really up to something here. He is just really blessing us. When you add this to what just happened with the amended tax returns, it is amazing."

Just a few weeks earlier, as I was preparing for the move, I came across copies of the last few years of tax returns. As I was getting ready to box them up, the Lord stopped me.

"Vicki, I want you to amend your last two tax returns. You left money sitting on the table. Let me show you your mistakes and just how much money you have coming back."

I was surprised to know that I had not done my tax returns right. I had always felt confident in doing my own returns. My Mom always did her and Dad's returns. It was not all that hard, once you had done it a few times. I had been doing our tax returns for over 13 years.

"Okay, Lord. If You are sure, I will take the time to look them over again right now." As I studied the returns, I was embarrassed at the stupid mistakes I had made. Now that the Lord had brought it to my attention, the mistakes were obvious to me. It would have been different if it had been just once. I made stupid mistakes two years in a row. I never would have checked the returns again if the Holy Spirit had not spoken to me so strongly.

When I had corrected the two returns, the Internal Revenue Service and New York State combined owed us $4,500. With the interest on the children's money, we had just earned $6,500 in one month. I was very glad I had believed and obeyed the Lord. He was definitely rewarding our obedience in tangible ways. Although we felt so blessed in so many ways, cash was the one thing we never had much of. Only He knew how much we needed it.

"Thank you, Lord," I said, hugging myself. "I think this is going to be a very good year." Even I could not have imagined all He had in store for us.

It took us five days to drive from Rochester to Dallas. The first day, I was only able to drive a few hours. I was so exhausted, I just could not keep my heavy eyes open. The last few days before we left New York, I was up until 2:00 in the morning packing and cleaning. With five children, two of them under two, this move had drained everything from me.

We drove into Dallas on my 35th birthday. It had been four years since we had left. In some ways, it seemed like it was just yesterday. In other ways, it seemed like it had been an eternity.

I immediately organized myself and started calling agencies to look for work for Paco. We were excited about starting a freelance business, but we definitely did not feel prepared to start our own business just yet. Both of us enjoyed the security of a paycheck and benefits. Before Paco accepted the job in Rochester, we had never even had health insurance. I knew God Himself had protected us through our first four pregnancies and births.

I had a favorable response to my cold calls, and was able to line up over twenty interviews for Paco over a month's time. During that month, while we were hanging around the house waiting to hear back from one of the agencies Paco had interviewed with, we were to learn yet another lesson in obedience.

It was about 4:00 on a weekday afternoon, when I had an overwhelming urge to go to Sam's Club. I didn't know at the time that it was the Holy Spirit speaking to me. I just knew I had to go right then.

Paco looked at me strangely. "Vicki, we don't need anything from Sam's. Why do you want to go?"

"I don't know why. I just do. Come on, Paco. Nothing else is going on. Let's just go."

"Okay, whatever you say." We packed our two little sons in the car and drove to Sam's Club. It was about ten minutes from our house. Once we got there, we had just gotten the two boys strapped in two different carts and had started down the first aisle, when I had an overwhelming urge to leave.

"Honey, we have to leave right now," I said in an adamant tone of voice. I picked up one of the boys and he picked up the other one.

"You are crazy, Vic," Paco muttered under his breath. I could tell he was not happy with the situation. "First you have to come and then you have to leave. What is this all about, anyway?"

"I don't know, Paco. Please trust me. It is just something I know in my spirit, but cannot put into words. We had to come and we had to leave. Just like we did. I don't know why."

It didn't take us long to find out why. Just minutes later, as we were driving home on a very busy, four lane highway, we pulled up next to a semi pulling a crane. I was just staring out the window, studying the crane, when it suddenly came unhooked. The semi had gone over a small hump in the road, just enough to cause the crane to come loose. Within seconds, the crane started lifting up until it was in an almost upright position.

"Paco," I yelled. "Look."

"Oh my God," Paco said. "If we don't stop that driver right now, he is going to crash into that bridge." We both looked ahead of us at the overpass that was coming up on us quickly. There was a line of cars stopped on the overpass, waiting for a light to change. It was rush hour traffic on the interstate, and all of the lanes were packed with vehicles.

I rolled down my window and Paco pulled up next to the driver and started honking his horn wildly. I don't know if the driver was listening to music or just lost in his own thoughts, but he was not responding. We were so much lower than he was, he didn't even look down.

"Jesus," I screamed as we were rapidly coming up to the over-pass. "Help us, Jesus!" I stuck my head and hands out the window and flailed them frantically. Paco was laying on the horn. Finally, the man looked down at me and rolled down his window. I started pointing up at the crane while screaming for him to pull his truck over. He slowed way down, and started to pull over until he was finally on the shoulder. His truck had stopped just about twenty feet from the overpass.

Paco and I just looked at each other, completely traumatized by what had just happened. "Paco," I said slowly. "Do you realize we never would have been out in this traffic if we had not gone to Sam's this afternoon? And we definitely would not have been next to this truck when the crane came unhooked if we didn't leave when we did?"

"Vicki," Paco said. "Do you have any idea how many lives would have been lost if that crane had hit that overpass?"

We were both quiet the rest of the way home, just thinking about what might have been, if we had not been obedient to the Holy Spirit's prompting. I just kept remembering the overwhelming urge I had, and how I knew I had to do what I felt. I didn't know when I went to Sam's that we would be leaving immediately. I just knew that I was to go. And when I felt such a strong urge to leave, I didn't know that we were going to be instrumental in saving so many lives. I just knew we were to leave.

"Lord, help me to always take the higher road in the spirit. Help me to always recognize Your voice and to never be too busy to listen and obey. Thank You, Lord, for using Paco and me today. Please continue to use us for Your service."

On April 4, Paco dragged in from his latest interview. He had just been told that the agency owner felt he was overqualified for the opening. As he came in and sat down at the breakfast table, I could feel his pain. He was really down. The rejection was really getting to him.

"What is wrong with me, honey?" Paco asked gingerly. "I thought I was good. I am really beginning to doubt my ability. Nobody wants to hire me. We have got to do something soon. Our unemployment check doesn't even pay our house payment."

I had been sitting across the table from him, studying his downcast demeanor. I couldn't remember ever seeing Paco so down. With the exception of Pacquito's death, he had always been able to overcome obstacles without letting the drain get to him. This was different. It was as if he had lost his self-esteem. He was questioning the essence of who he was as a man. It disturbed me to see him so depressed.

Suddenly, I had a brainstorm. Before I even thought, I spoke. It was as if the Lord just bypassed my brain and went straight to my mouth. "Honey, let's forget about working for other agencies. You are just giving your talent away. I think it is time to birth 'The Garza Creative Group', don't you? Let's just start our own business. I think we should do it today."

"Today?" Paco looked at me in a daze. "What are you saying, Vicki?"

"I am saying we should go to the county courthouse and get our name registered, then get busy looking for a place to office. We will need to find a daycare for the boys and open a checking account. You know. All of the things that people do when they start a business. Let's just do it."

"Vicki," Paco responded. "Do you have any idea what you are saying? Once I stop looking for a job and start my own business, I have to discontinue unemployment benefits. How are we going to make it financially?"

"Paco," I said, frustration creeping into my voice. I stopped for a few seconds to add drama. It seemed to work. He was listening. "Don't you remember the prophecy God gave us on the eighth anniversary of Pacquito's death? That was His promise to us. He said He would go before us and that He would promote us. He said He would give us an advertising agency that would bring glory to His name. I know it is a huge step of faith, sweetheart. But if we ever needed the Lord, we need Him now. I think we need to seize the day and move forward in faith." I could actually see the despair lifting off his spirit. His face reflected a glimmer of hope.

"Do you really believe 'The Garza Creative Group's' time has come, Vic?"

"Yes, darling, I really do. Let's stop talking and go to the courthouse. We've got a lot to do today if we are going to start a business." I dropped the boys off at Mother's Day Out and we left for downtown Dallas.

As we walked out of the courthouse with our assumed name certificate, we both felt so much more confident about our future. It felt great to have hope and to be moving forward in faith with a God-given plan. Paco squeezed my hand affectionately. "Did you ever think we would be business partners, honey? So many people say they can't work with their spouse. Do you think you can work with me?"

I looked at him and winked. "Oh, I think maybe I can suffer through. How about you? Do you think you can work with me?

Paco did not hesitate. "Vicki. I can't think of anyone I would rather work with. I think you are everything I am not and vice-versa. We complement each other perfectly."

I had not thought about it that much, but it was true. We were perfectly matched. Although we had each had our own businesses, we had never actually been equal partners in business together. "This will be interesting," I thought. "I wonder if we will still enjoy working together ten years from now."

That night, after Paco fell asleep, I got before the Lord with my feelings about leaving my two baby boys in daycare. John had turned two in February and Daniel had turned one. They were still so little and sweet. I honestly could not imagine dropping them off somewhere for the day and picking them up at night. I loved being home with all of my children. Being home with the babies was extra special. Since I had older children, I had a special appreciation for the two youngest, which I knew would grow up all too soon.

"Lord, I do not know if I can do this," I choked. "You know how my heart is breaking. Who can I trust to love and care for my boys the way I do? We don't know anyone. How can I just leave them with strangers?"

Hot tears streamed down my cheeks. The emotional pain of leaving my babies to re-enter the workforce was gut wrenching. Breaking into bitter sobs, I cried until I felt I could cry no more. Paco slept soundly beside of me, snoring with rhythmic precision. I will never forget that night, as I pled with the Lord to please make another way for His will to be accomplished in our lives. I identified with what Jesus must have felt in the garden of Gethsemane, when He asked for the cup to be passed from Him. He knew if He went forward with the plan, it would mean His crucifixion. Although my suffering was miniscule compared to what Jesus suffered, I did know that starting our own business would mean crucifying my flesh. The pain was just beginning. I knew the struggle would be long and hard and agonizing. Worst of all, I knew I had no choice but to proceed if I wanted the Lord to continue to bless my family and me.

"Oh God," I begged. "Please give me the strength to do this. Your strength is made perfect in my weakness. I know You can carry me through this difficult time."

The next day I started to make my calls for daycares and set up interviews to see if the home daycare was right for us. After interviewing the first home daycare, we had perfect confidence the Lord would give us peace when we found the care provider He had chosen for us. I struck gold on the second try. The moment I met "Miss Violet," I knew she was the one. She and her husband ran a daycare from their home. I could tell as I looked at all of the sweet, joyful faces of the children she kept she was a good and loving provider. I was right. She and her husband were God's gift to our family.

Once the boys were in daycare, we had time to really roll up our sleeves and get to work. Within a week, we had moved into a 12 x 12 office space we could rent for $350 a month or barter the rent for work. The office was filled with displaced creative professionals who all had the same deal. The concept was great. Since everyone shared a common receptionist and conference room, it was like having your own agency without the entire overhead. We were able to get business cards printed, our bank accounts opened and the essentials we needed to be in business. We joined councils and got membership lists. Within the first week, I went to a networking event that was heavily attended by local Fortune 500 Companies.

One of the individuals I met our first week in business turned out to be our way into Texas Instruments four years later. I was determined to sow good seeds, water them faithfully and patiently wait for my harvest. I knew as we sowed we would also reap. Since we were very hungry, we sowed lots of seeds.

The first thing I did was type up a plaque with a scripture paraphrased from Zechariah: "Do not despise the day of small beginnings." I hung it in our office and waited for God to move. Everyday was filled with anticipation.

One day, shortly after we had started the business, I had another one of those strange urges come over me. "Honey, we need to go to the grocery store."

"Do you need something, Vic?"

"No. Not really. I just really feel like we are supposed to go. Come on!"

Paco was getting used to my whims and climbed into the

driver's seat like a good sport. When we got out of our car and started walking toward the store, we spotted an old friend from Church on the Rock.

"Caroline," Paco and I both cried with enthusiasm. "How *are* you?"

It had been over four years since we had seen Caroline and her husband, Dave. They knew everyone on staff at the church, so she was able to fill us in on what had become of them. Just before we got ready to say goodbye, she started asking us questions.

"So what are you all up to these days?" she asked, with a sincere interest. "Are you doing alright?"

We explained our situation and told her we were very actively looking for leads for our business.

"Listen," Caroline said. "This is my bosses card. He knows a lot of people. Call him and ask him if he knows of anyone that might need some design work. I am pretty sure he can give you a few good leads."

"Thanks, Caroline," I said enthusiastically. "I will definitely give him a call."

We hugged Caroline and she walked to her car. Then Paco turned to me and asked, "Did you need something from Albertson's, Vic?"

"Nope," I said beaming. "I just got what I came for."

That is the way the Lord worked in our lives that year. That single lead led to our very first ad with Sky Chefs in June. The same day we picked up an ad from the marketing director of Bank One. The Sky Chefs lead eventually led to several large marketing projects over the next few years.

With our first client check of $3,250 we bought a used Macintosh computer. Within weeks we were enrolled in continuing education classes to learn the essential software programs. By September, we were fully functional on the computer and leading the way technologically in our industry. Because the big agencies were so slow to hop on the digital bandwagon, we were able to run circles around them in price and efficiency.

It was hard to believe we had only been in Dallas for six short months. We found a wonderful sublease space we could afford and began to establish ourselves as an advertising agency.

By the time the year was out, we had billed over $70,000. Although more than half of that figure represented our overhead and outside costs, we were amazed at what God had done with our simple, childlike faith. I could not help but remember how we ached to have a paycheck with benefits and just laughed. God's way was so much more exciting.

Those first few years were hard, without a doubt. Many nights and weekends, we had to go back to work as we struggled to meet deadlines. We were not charging nearly enough for our work, so we had to work twice as hard to make as much as others in our industry. As a means of showcasing our talent, we would often give our work away by creating pro-bono ad campaigns. The strategy worked and the word was spreading that we were fast and cheap. But with five children under the age of twelve, we were regularly burning the candle at both ends.

Our first big break came in October 1992. We still had not been able to incorporate or take salaries from our business, since we kept investing as much as possible back into the business and taking money out as we needed it for our home bills.

TU Electric had called our agency to create an ad earlier in the summer. They liked our work so much they decided to include us in a Request for Proposal for all of the company's Hispanic advertising. Since they were using an established Hispanic agency, and we had no Hispanic advertising experience, I knew the odds were slim to none.

I also knew I served a mighty God. "Lord, You know what this win could mean for us. It could put us on the map in Dallas and give us the springboard we need to showcase our creative talents. Please, Lord, be glorified through us. Let Your power be seen through our agency." Miraculously, our little 2-man shop was chosen as the new agency of record for TU Electric's Hispanic advertising. The same month, we incorporated and started taking bi-weekly salaries. A few months later, we signed ourselves up for health insurance.

The next few years were a blur. We worked hard, and eventually, instead of subleasing, we could sign our own lease in a high-rise in the Uptown area of Dallas.

True to His Word, the Lord was establishing us as a viable ad agency. By the time we started hiring full time employees, we had already won several impressive chamber, client and industry awards. As the word spread of our high standards of excellence, we were able to bring glory to His name. Our agency's success was clearly supernatural.

> *"And though the Lord gives you the bread of adversity and the water of affliction, yet your Teacher will not hide Himself anymore, but your eyes will constantly behold your Teacher. And your ears will hear a word behind you, saying, This is the way, walk in it, when you turn to the right hand and when you turn to the left."*
>
> *Isaiah 30:20,21*

CHAPTER 13

Abortion Intervention

∽

In January 1994, I had another one of those sudden urges. I had no idea, at that time, how much God was moving behind the scenes to get me where He wanted me to be. Paco and I had spent the morning with a nurse who came to our offices to take our blood pressure and weight and took blood samples for testing for the life insurance company. At lunch, I had a sudden inspiration. It seemed to come out of nowhere.

"You know, honey, we both have been steadily gaining weight over the past few years. We work too hard and don't have time to exercise regularly. I know we were talking about trying to take a cruise this winter, but I don't know how we will be able to get away from our kids or business to do that. I think it would cost less than $1,000 for us to get a membership at the health club. Why don't we use our money there instead of on a vacation? It really makes more sense and is a better lifestyle decision. What do you think?"

Paco was agreeable to the idea. "Sounds good to me. Why don't you find out how much it costs and a little more about it and we will see?"

"Honey, the health club is just down the street. Why don't we just go over there right now and tour the facilities and hear the sales pitch?"

Within the hour, Paco and I were sitting in the health club

manager's office looking over contracts and asking questions.

"I have a question," I said matter-of-factly. "What ages do you take in the nursery?"

"What ages are your children?" the young, redheaded manager asked. "We can probably accommodate them."

"We have five children, ages four to fourteen."

The manager was obviously taken aback. "You two have five children? I cannot believe that," she gasped. "You seem so young and professional. I never would have guessed you are a mother of five," she said, looking at me with genuine admiration. "I am impressed." After a pause, she regained her composure.

I was wearing the new gold Christian fish symbol Paco had bought me for Christmas around my neck. Suddenly, I was aware of it. I reached my hand up to finger it. I had a strong impression this was a perfect opportunity to witness to this woman.

"When we first got married, I could not imagine myself as a mother. I felt totally unprepared to be anyone's mom. Then I gave my life to Christ. That single decision changed my life. The Lord has given us both the ability to be successful parents, as well as successful professionals. It was the single most important decision we ever made."

She was really listening closely to what I had to say. I could tell she was thinking about it, but the time didn't seem right to pursue it. I decided to change the subject.

"Well, we need to be getting back to the office. Paco and I will sit down and discuss these contracts and pricing and see if the membership fees fit within our budget. I will be calling you or coming by tomorrow if we decide to do this."

We excused ourselves and left the club. On the way back to the office, we discussed the incident. Paco felt as strongly as I did that we had just come from a divine appointment. By the time we got back to the office, we already knew we wanted to join the club.

"I will just wait and go in tomorrow after lunch with the checks and the contracts," I said enthusiastically. "Aren't you excited, Paco? We are going to lose weight and get in shape, just like we planned. I cannot wait to get started!"

The next day after lunch, I stopped by the club. When the elevator opened, the manager was standing there. When she saw me, she looked like she had seen a ghost.

"Vicki!"

"Hi there. How are you today?"

"I am fine. Please come with me. I have something I have to tell you."

She hurriedly walked me back to her office and shut the door. Immediately, she began to pour her heart out to me. "I have a story to tell you that you will not believe. First of all, I want to tell you that I spent a lot of time with my grandmother growing up. She was a very strong Christian woman. She prayed in tongues and everything. So I was exposed to a lot of Christian experiences in my formative years. Over the years, those memories became dimmer and dimmer to me until I had all but forgotten them. As a teenager, I had several bad relationships. I think that hardened me to a lot of things.

My husband and I have not been married that long and were hoping to work awhile before we had children. It completely took us by surprise when we discovered I was pregnant. We had a long talk about it and had decided that this just was not the right time to have a baby. So I called a doctor to get an abortion. I was supposed to have my abortion yesterday afternoon.

When you and your husband came in yesterday and said you had five children, I could not believe it. All I could think about was my grandma and the things she taught me. I knew she would want me to have the baby and raise it in a good, Christian home. After you left, I called my husband and we decided we were going to do the right thing and have the baby. After that, I called the doctor and canceled my abortion appointment. We believe God wants our baby to be born."

I was at a loss for words. I was so touched by her story. "I am so glad. You will not regret your decision, I promise. Let's pray right now and ask the Lord to protect this baby in your womb. And when you have your baby, you come by and visit me, okay? I would like to pray over you and your baby and dedicate that baby to the Lord."

As I was leaving, we stood at the door and hugged. "Please continue to pray for me, Vicki, okay? It is hard to be a pregnant manager at a health club. The management was pretty upset with me when I told them this morning."

"I will pray. I promise."

Once we realized the Lord's true purpose for our health club membership, we didn't care if we got our money's worth or not. After a few weeks, we hardly went anymore. As far as we were concerned, our membership had purchased a child's life.

It was nearly a year and a half before I saw her again. True to her word, she stopped by one day with her little son and let me pray for him. "Vicki, I wanted you to know that we think about you and Paco often and thank God that you guys came into our lives when you did. We love our son so much. We cannot believe how close we came to losing him. Also, my husband wanted me to tell you that we are having Bible studies in our home weekly. We have found a wonderful church and our group is growing."

"Wow," I said, trying to hold back the tears. "I think of you often as well. There is no doubt in my mind the Lord had a special mission for us the day we came to the health club for a membership. Isn't God just so good? He continually amazes me."

> *"Before I formed you in the womb, I knew [and] approved of you [as my chosen instrument], and before you were born, I separated and set you apart, consecrating you...."*
>
> *Jeremiah 1:5*

> *"Behold, children are a heritage from the Lord, the fruit of the womb a reward. As arrows are in the hand of a warrior, so are the children of one's youth. Happy, blessed, and fortunate is the man whose quiver is filled with them."*
>
> *Psalm 127:3-5*

CHAPTER 14

The Blessing Seat

❦

I n August of that same year, I attended a function at Hillcrest church, where we had been attending since Easter Sunday, 1993. The seminar ran for three weeknights. The first two nights, I had gone straight to the front and sat in the same chair both nights. I had always preferred to sit up close, so as not to be distracted by people in front of me. The third night, I was heading for my usual seat, when the Holy Spirit stopped me.

"Don't sit where you have been sitting. Sit over there tonight, by the older blonde woman."

"Okay, Lord. Whatever you say." I hated to make everyone stand up so that I could squeeze through when there were so many other seats open, but I knew I had to obey. I plopped myself down by the older, blonde woman and promptly introduced myself.

"Hi. I'm Vicki Garza."

"Nice to meet you, Vicki. I'm Jane Olsen."

We sat and talked for a few minutes before the session started. I was impressed when she told me that she was the President of the Dallas Chapter of Women's Aglow.

"Wow," I thought. "She must be very strong in the Lord."

At some point early on in the session, the speaker asked us to take hands. When I took Jane's hand, her reaction was immediate. Moving closer to me to whisper in my ear, she said, "Vicki, did you know you have the gift of healing?"

I nodded my head, to let her know I did.

After the service was over, Jane turned to me. "Vicki," she said. "I have such a strong witness in my spirit that the Lord wants to use you mightily in business. I assume you own a business, correct?"

"Oh, yes. I do. I own an ad agency with my husband."

"This is the word the Lord wants me to give to you tonight."

"I am pleased with you my child. You have been faithful in the little things. Now I know I can trust you to be faithful over much. What you have witnessed in your business is just the beginning of what I desire to do with you. Take time out now and prepare for the new business I have set aside for you. It will require systems that you do not yet have. Be diligent to upgrade your internal systems now, so when the business comes, you will be prepared. Move quickly for the time is short."

I looked at Jane in amazement. I had never met her before and would not have met her if the Holy Spirit had not changed my seat. Yet, I knew in my heart that her word was from the Lord. I did as the Lord asked and began upgrading our internal processes.

Through an unusual series of events, 7-Eleven called our agency in to design and illustrate a calendar for all of their franchisees. It required a significant investment on our part in memory and hardware to be able to complete the job, the way they wanted it done digitally. The job was given to us in mid-September. When we had successfully finished the job, the brand manager asked the legal department to draw up an agency of record contract for our agency. We signed it on October 5th, just about six weeks from the time the prophecy was spoken over me. Once again, the Lord had been faithful to keep His Word. He was promoting us in ways we never thought possible.

The following year, we added Texas Instruments to our client roster. We went from doing several odd jobs for them, to over 400 jobs a year for several years. Now that we had three significant clients, our agency was quickly growing. There did not seem to be enough hours in the day for all I had to do. My job description was so broad, there was nothing at the agency I did not have my hand on at all times. Paco loved the luxury of being in charge of the creative content of all of the projects, so the hiring and firing, billing and paying, job supervision and project management fell under my charge. I was also responsible for all new business for the agency.

When I look back on those years, I honestly do not know how I was able to handle everything at the office, in addition to the responsibilities of being a mother to five children ranging in age from five to fifteen. Before my oldest could drive, I was dropping off my three oldest children at three different public schools – one at the high school, one at the middle school and one at the elementary school. Then, I would drop off the two little boys at their home daycare. By 3:30, I reversed the cycle and picked them all up from three different schools and the boys from their daycare provider.

That year, I did not have any outside help in cleaning my home. And, of course, I was also in charge of overseeing the laundry, meals, shopping, and getting the children to their events after school. I know the only way I was able to do all that I did, and remain sane, was by the power of the Holy Spirit. Many times I felt like a single parent again. Although Paco was more than willing to help me at home, he was never there. He was spending every waking moment at work, meeting the ever-increasing demands and deadlines of the multiple projects from various clients. It was a dizzying time.

> *"She girds herself with strength [spiritual, mental and physical fitness for her God-given task] and makes her arms strong and firm. She tastes and sees that her gain from work [with and for God] is good; her lamp goes not out, but it burns on continually through the night [of trouble, privation, or sorrow, warning away fear, doubt and distrust]."*
>
> *Proverbs 31: 17,18*

CHAPTER 15

The Miracle Of
The Kidney Stone

⨯

By January of 1996, the stress and pressure of working 80 to 100 hour weeks finally caught up with Paco: In mid-January, he had his first kidney stone attack. Unfortunately, the stone was stubborn and refused to pass. Paco spent the weekend in the hospital, with a dispenser of morphine attached to him by an IV to kill the pain. By Sunday night, the stone had repositioned itself and he was back at work by Monday morning. Oddly enough, this scene replayed itself every four weeks for six months. Every fourth Saturday, he was back in the hospital and back home by Sunday night. After about the third episode, I told Paco I wanted to speak with his doctor personally the next time he had an appointment. After the doctor was finished examining him, I asked him if I could ask a few questions.

The urologist became very defensive as I questioned him about the procedure to be followed when a kidney stone would not budge. He assured me that if Paco would just drink a 6-pack of beer every weekend, he would be able to pass the stone. When I told him we did not drink beer, he said that was our problem. His flippant attitude was unprofessional and disturbing. When I asked him if he would please consider removing the stone surgically, he refused to even consider surgery as an option. Due to the location of the stone, it could not be broken up by sonar. So, the doctor concluded, Paco would basically have to sweat it out until the stone passed. When we left his office that day, I was furious. One way or another, the situation had to be rectified. Paco could not live like this. It was wreaking havoc on him, as well as the rest of us.

By the time I was able to discuss the situation in detail with the urologist's supervisor and have Paco removed from his care and put under the care of another urologist, it was another couple of months. By mid-June, when Paco had his sixth attack since January, the decision was made on the spot by another doctor to remove the stone surgically. Paco had finally gotten the relief for which he had so desperately prayed.

At the time, we questioned the Lord as to why He would make Paco go through such pain and suffering. We had laid hands on Paco and prayed for the Lord to move the stone many times. Although the Lord did not answer us at the time, He did make the answer crystal clear three years later. When He finally revealed the purpose, it made shivers run right up and down both of our spines. The final twist to the story is too bizarre to believe.

In the fall of 1998, our high-rise office lease had come up for renewal. The building management was hiking the rate from $14 a square foot to $24 a square foot and wanted a five-year lease. With 3,600 square feet of space, that represented a considerable commitment on our part that we did not feel prepared to meet. After analyzing our options and asking the Lord for direction, we felt led to purchase an old historic house in the Uptown area of Dallas.

To assist with the sizeable down payment that purchase would require, we decided to sell the rent home we had been leasing out since1984. I had called our renters to see if they would be interested in buying the house. I was fairly certain they would, since she had mentioned how much they loved the house and would like to buy it if we ever decided to sell it. If the sale was as easy as it seemed, we could do a 1031 Exchange and defer income tax on the sale. The proceeds from the one property would just roll over into this new property and we would save over $20k by not having to report the sale as a gain. It seemed to be a very wise thing to do.

"Patricia," I said, when I got her on the phone. "You know how you and Steve have been wanting to buy the house you are renting? Paco and I have put a purchase offer in on another property and would like to sell that house to you to use the proceeds as a part of the down payment on our new property. Did you guys want to buy the house?"

After I told her the price (a real deal with no commissions involved), she was elated. "Vicki," she said. "I will talk to Steve about it right away, but I can assure you, we do want to buy the house. We love this neighborhood and our kids love their schools. We would not want to live anywhere else. We have even got the money in our savings to make it happen right away. We have both been at our jobs for years, so that won't be a problem. I would say you could count on us to sign on the dotted line."

"That is great, Patricia. Paco and I will stop by with a real estate contract tomorrow and we will get the whole process rolling. Do you have any contingencies?"

She was quiet for a moment, then said, "Just a financing contingency, I guess. But I cannot imagine that would be a problem."

When we finished talking, I was excited. Everything was going exactly according to plan. The timing should fall right into place so that everything would work out perfectly. We were closing on the new property in mid-January, so that gave us all plenty of time to pull our paperwork together.

Over the next sixty days, Patricia called me repeatedly to report on the progress of their financing. Finally, shortly after New Year's, she called in tears. "Vicki, I am so frustrated. This has been the most exasperating experience of my life. We have done everything the financing people have asked." She began to run down the list of requests, and their appropriate responses. It seemed odd that Patricia was experiencing such stiff resistance.

Even as she was talking, a huge flag went up in my spirit. "Oh Lord," I thought. "They are not supposed to buy our house."

"Patricia," I said with authority. The urgent tone of my voice caught her off guard.

"What?" she asked sheepishly.

"I just realized you guys are not supposed to buy the house."

"How do you know that?" she asked.

"Because the Holy Spirit just revealed it to me. The Lord has another house for you and Steve. When you do everything you are supposed to do and you keep running up against a brick wall, that could mean that you are not in God's perfect will. You don't want to be out of His perfect will, do you?"

"No, no. Of course we don't."

"Do you mind if I pray with you right now, Patricia, and ask the Lord to reveal Himself to you and Steve? We will just pray that God will lead you to the perfect home of His choosing for your family. Let's just ask him to give you peace and wisdom and divine guidance. Would that be okay?"

"Oh yes. Of course it would."

By the time we hung up, I had a new best friend. Patricia was thankful that I had prayed with her and helped her to see that it was more important to be in God's will than to buy our house.

Although the decision meant we would have to forego the 1031 Exchange and pay the $20k capital gains tax on the house, it was worth it to know that God was in charge of who would live in our home. We put it on the market and it sold several months after we closed on our historic home in Uptown. Fortunately, we were able to pay the down payment without the income from the rental home, so nothing was lost.

In mid-April, I got a frantic phone call from Patricia.

"Vicki," she said quickly. "This is Patricia. Do you have a minute to talk?"

"Of course I do, Patricia." I was alarmed by the panic I could sense in her voice.

"I know you are a Christian and that you know how to pray. I just could not think of anyone else to call."

She told me that she and her twelve-year old daughter had just come from the urologist's office and had been told that her daughter would have to undergo an experimental, life-threatening surgery to have one of her kidneys removed. The doctor wanted to operate immediately and had told Patricia there was no time to get a second opinion.

"Wait a minute, Patricia. We use the same HMO you do and we have had very real concerns about the competency of one of the urologists. Paco had a six-month bout with a kidney stone that could have been avoided if the doctor had been doing his job. Which urologist did you meet with today?"

When she told me, I was horrified. It was the same doctor with which we had dealt. He was the only doctor on whom I had ever filed a formal complaint.

"Listen to me, Patricia," I said with absolute authority. "Under no circumstance do you let that man touch your daughter. He is incompetent and should not be practicing medicine. Promise me you will take your daughter to another doctor and will not let this man touch her."

"I promise," she said. Her voice was shaking. "I kept thinking that something was not quite right about him. He kept referring to a new, experimental surgery that he wanted to perform on our daughter. It was so new and experimental that if he should succeed, he would be one of the first doctors to ever perform it successfully. It just seemed like he was much more interested in getting to use our daughter as a guinea pig for his new technique than he was in her health."

Before we hung up that day, I prayed with Patricia that the Lord would continue to order her steps. She promised me she would call as soon as she could with the outcome of the situation.

In about a week, Patricia called to tell me what had happened with her daughter. The very next morning, she had taken her daughter to see another urologist. He suggested her daughter receive the traditional kidney surgery to have one kidney removed. When Patricia told him the procedure the other urologist wanted to perform on her daughter, the doctor was aghast. He suggested that he ask the first urologist to assist him in the traditional surgery so he could see for himself what would have happened if he had attempted the riskier surgery. The surgery had gone very well and her daughter was recovering beautifully.

Shortly after the surgery, the surgeon called Patricia into his office to speak with her. He informed Patricia that without a doubt, if the first urologist had performed the experimental surgery, her daughter would have hemorrhaged to death. He was pleased with the satisfaction of knowing he was able to save her daughter as well as teach the other urologist a lesson he would not have learned any other way.

After our phone conversation, I thought long and hard about all of the steps that had to happen for the Lord to perform this miracle. It all started with the awful renters we had before Patricia and Steve. They turned out to be traveling rip-off artists that were stealing expensive cars and disassembling them in our garage. By the time the police were on to them, they had skipped out on us, leaving past rent due, as well as a terrible mess to clean up. Once I got the house ready to rent again, I had decided that I would take my time finding good tenants and that I would be more careful to do a background check. Although the process did take quite a bit longer, it was well worth it, since Patricia and Steve were some of the best tenants we had ever had.

If we had not decided to buy the new property for office space, we never would have asked Patricia and Steve to buy our house. If the credit union had not given them such a hard time, Patricia and I never would have prayed on the phone and she would not have known I was a Christian. And if Paco had not gone through six months of living hell with his kidney stone, we never would have even known the incompetent urologist.

Of all of the miracles God has performed in our lives, this one is so special to us, because it cost us so much. Although Paco had to endure six weekends of mind-numbing pain and we paid out many thousands of dollars in income taxes, lost rent and property damage, it was such a small price to pay for a girl to have life.

"Behold, the Lord's eye is upon those who fear Him [who revere and worship Him with awe], who wait for Him and hope in His mercy and loving-kindness, to deliver them from death and keep them alive in famine. Our inner selves wait [earnestly] for the Lord; He is our help and our Shield. For in Him does our heart rejoice, because we have trusted (relied on and been confident) in His holy name. Let your loving-kindness, Oh Lord, be upon us, in proportion to our waiting and hoping for You."
Psalm 33:18-22

CHAPTER 16

The Year Of Promotion

⌘

Without a doubt, 1999 was God's year of promotion for me personally. I had been asked to serve as a Board Member on the Greater Dallas Chamber of Commerce in late1998, and my service began with the first meeting in January. As I sat in the huge conference room with all of the other Board Members, I looked around at the corporate giants in the room with me. Out of 33 Board Members, 28 came from Fortune 1000 companies. The other five (including me) were from small and mid-size businesses.

The same month, I was selected by Working Woman Magazine as one of six female entrepreneurs from a 4-state region to win an Award of Excellence. My award was for overcoming obstacles. This honor was especially dear to me, because I never would have entered the contest if the Lord had not commanded me to do so.

My banker had asked me to apply for the contest when the deadline was just a week away. I thanked her for the forms and after looking them over, decided there was no way I had time to write so many essays in such a short period of time. The day before the application had to be postmarked, I had a rare evening with nothing to do. My husband and children were out, and I was home alone. About 9:00, I thought, "I guess I will go to bed early tonight."

As I got up to go to bed, the Lord spoke to me clearly: "Vicki, you did not even ask me if you were supposed to apply for the

Working Woman award. You need to get started on it now and finish it by tomorrow evening, when you can FedEx it."

"Oh no," I moaned. "You know how I hate filling out forms, Lord. Those essay questions were complicated. That application should take weeks. I am exhausted, Lord. Can't I please just go to bed?" The Holy Spirit was unrelenting. I knew I had no choice but to obey.

When Paco and the kids came home, I was sitting at the computer typing frantically. "What are you working on, Vic? I didn't know you brought work home with you tonight," Paco said as he walked through the door.

"Honey," I said. "The Lord just told me about an hour ago that I have to fill out this application my banker gave me for Working Woman Magazine. I will be up all night."

"See you tomorrow, sweetie. If the Lord said to do it, He must have had a reason."

I typed frantically into the wee hours of the morning. After a few hours of sleep, I got up and started typing where I had left off. By 8:00 that night, I was driving up to the FedEx center to drop off the package. I thought for sure they closed at 8:30. As I walked up to the door, the FedEx man was walking away. It was obvious he had just locked the door. I did not have any of the necessary packaging and labels, so it was very important to me that I get in. I could not just drop it in the box.

I tapped on the window. The man turned his back to me, ignoring me. I tapped again. There was still no response. Finally, I started to scream and beat the door. "Let me in. *Please* let me in. I have a very important document that has to be postmarked tonight. It is a contest I am entering. I have been working on it non-stop and just now finished. *Please* let me in. PLEASE!"

Finally, the man came over and unlocked the door. "That is one of the best excuses I have ever heard for getting the FedEx man to unlock the door."

"It is all true, I promise," I said as I hurriedly filled out the form. Once completed, I took it back to him. "See?" I said. "I am sending this to Working Woman Magazine in New York City."

"Now don't you forget that I am the man that helped you win.

You come back and thank me, you hear?" he teased as he threw my package in the bin.

"I promise, I will let you know. I think that you are my very own personal angel. I could not have done it without you."

Several months later, after my award was announced to a packed crowd of hopeful entrepreneurs from a four-state region, I returned to tell the FedEx man the good news. He just beamed. I was very pleased, as well. I never would have entered if the Holy Spirit had not urged me. That award proved to be a springboard to other promotions the Lord had in store for me that year.

In January 2000, I got a call from the business administrator from Hillcrest Church where we had been attending since 1993. "Vicki," she said. "A member of the congregation has nominated you to serve as a trustee for Hillcrest Church. The purpose of this phone call is to see if you would be interested in serving."

I told her I would definitely like to serve the church in that capacity, if the congregation elected me. As I hung up, my head was swimming. "Lord, you are so awesome. When you promised to promote me, I had no idea how you were going to do it."

Never in my wildest dreams did I ever imagine the Lord had so many honors in store for us. Over the years, we had won numerous industry awards, client awards and chamber awards. Our office walls were literally covered with awards. And yet, as I meditated on God's faithfulness, I felt very unworthy to receive such honor.

Sadly, although I was to be elected as a church trustee, serving on Chamber boards, winner of a Working Woman award, I was not fulfilled. I was at the pinnacle of my success and it was not enjoyable. It was this deep sense of unworthiness and lack of fulfillment that caused me to experience two of the most difficult years of my life emotionally. It was a very lonely place for me.

> *"But without faith it is impossible to please and be satisfactory to Him. For whoever would come near to God must [necessarily] believe that God exists and that He is the rewarder of those who earnestly and diligently seek Him [out]."*
>
> *Hebrews 11:6*

"Humble yourselves [feeling very insignificant] in the presence of the Lord, and He will exalt you [He will lift you up and make your lives significant].
James 4:10

CHAPTER 17

A Year Of New Beginnings

❧

By January of 2000, my loneliness was unbearable. On top of that, I was feeling lost and confused. On Martin Luther King Day, I drove the children around town, dropping them off at various places. Just running errands drained me. It seemed to be such a chore. I was in a real spiritual, emotional and mental slump and I just did not know how to pull myself up out of it. As I drove up to yet another store, I let the kids out and waited in the car, too weary and depressed to run inside. I reached for the yellow pad beside me and started writing a letter to the Lord.

From the depths of my personal pain, I asked the Lord to please release me to go home to be with Him. I was tired and unmotivated. Sensing that my purpose on earth was over, I begged God to take me to my heavenly home.

I wrote from the core of my being that day, pouring out all of my pain onto that yellow pad. I was tired as an entrepreneur, as a wife, as a mother and as a Christian. I was just plain tired of living. The daily routine of life had become so mundane and joyless. Looking back, it had been creeping up on me for nearly two years. The closer I got to the top, and the more material successes I experienced in my life, the less motivated I felt.

That evening, Paco and I rented a movie. When the movie was over, I decided to take it back to the video store. In all the years we had rented movies, I had never volunteered to go out late at night to return the video. Although it was past 11:30, I did not mind getting out on this particular night, since I felt like getting some fresh air. As I walked out the door, I stopped on our front patio and looked up into the sky. "The stars seem to be brighter than usual," I thought. "And the air is so still, it is almost eerie." I stood there for a minute, just breathing in the cold night air. Then I climbed into my car and started for the rental store.

As I came up to the first intersection, the light was red. I waited for the red light to change to green, deep in thought, contemplating my emotional day.

Just then, the Lord spoke to my spirit so loudly, I almost jumped: "Vicki, do not move when the green arrow comes on. Just wait for Me to tell you when to turn."

"Okay, Lord." I looked into my rear view mirror to see how many cars were behind me. There were several. When the green arrow came on, I began to feel anxious.

"Lord," I said. "These people are all waiting for me to turn. When can I go?" I was nervously checking my rearview mirror, feeling really guilty about making the line behind me wait.

Just then, a black truck going at least 70 mph sped through the intersection. My heart leapt, as I realized that I would have been directly in his path. I was sure I would have been killed on impact.

My body began to shake, as I realized how quickly my life would have been taken from the earth. When I got to the video store, I looked over at the yellow pad, still stuck between the seats. "Oh Lord," I thought. "Thank You for unanswered prayer. You must still have a purpose for me after all."

As I ran up the steps to our house with the yellow pad tucked under my arm, I told Paco the entire story. His eyes filled with tears, as I told him how God had just saved my life. And how much I had wanted to die that day.

"I still need you, honey" he said, drawing me close. "Do not ever think I do not need you." I just buried my head into his chest and cried. I knew that he did need me. It felt great just to be alive and to be needed, not only by Paco, but also by God.

"Now tear up that letter to God, Vicki. Just imagine if you had been killed and that letter had been next to you."

I had goose bumps just thinking about it.

Just a few weeks later, on February 3rd, I had a breakfast meeting with a dear friend who was also the Chairman of the Board of the Greater Dallas Chamber. As Albert and I sat talking, he addressed me directly: "Vicki, I know you. There is something different about you. It is almost like you are depressed or something. What is going on with you?"

"What do you mean, Albert? I am not depressed. Nothing is going on with me."

"Well, maybe that is the problem. Nothing is going on with you. Ever since I have known you, there has always been something going on. What projects are you working on right now?"

"We have been pretty slow, Albert. I am not really working on any projects right now. I am just doing routine administrative work and my general duties of overseeing the agency. It has been pretty slow for awhile now."

"Come on, now, Vicki. You are more of a go-getter than that. Go out there and get yourself some business. Dallas is a big city and Garza Communications is really good. Why don't you have any business?"

I had all kinds of excuses for Albert that morning, but he was not buying any of them. The more excuses I made, the more adamant he became that we should be busier than we were.

"Change your name if you have to. Come on, Vicki. You are a marketing expert. Re-invent yourself. Get with the times. This is the era of 'dot com everything'. Can you do 'dot com' stuff?"

"Of course we can, Albert. Advertising is advertising. We can probably do 'dot com' better than the large agencies. We are leaner and meaner and smaller and faster."

"How do I know that, Vicki? Your name doesn't tell me that you are any of those things. I will tell you what. I have some homework for you. I want you to be thinking of a new name for your agency. Give Garza Communications a new twist and find a way to market yourself to all of those clients that are going crazy trying to figure out how they can spend their money to get a piece of the 'dot com' action."

As we parted ways that morning, I promised Albert I would do as he asked. I would be seriously thinking of ways to re-invent our agency to market it to the many clients that were literally clamoring at the doors of big agencies to get a piece of the 'dot com' pie.

The next morning, February 4th, I awoke at 4:00 a.m. with "The Dot Com Agency" practically burning in my brain. I jumped out of bed and ran to the Internet to do a search. To my amazement, the name was still available. My spirit surged as I got out my credit card and secured "thedotcomagency.com" on the domain registration site. By 10:00 a.m., I had spoken with my attorney and secured the corporate name in Texas, then applied for a trademark for the federal rights to the name. We were onto something big and I knew it.

Over the next few months, our office was buzzing with activity. I bet everything we had on the new identity, as I committed our entire personal savings account to the project. Paco was on board 100 percent. Although he did not pretend to understand, he had learned over the years to trust my intuition. If I believed God had given me a special opportunity or idea, Paco was always quick to get behind me and support me in it. I was more convinced than ever that God must have searched the earth to find Paco specifically for me. No other man would have allowed me the freedom to be what the Lord had called me to be.

My good friend Greta called one day to get a quick update on the new venture. When I told her what all had been accomplished, and the people God was putting in my path, she was amazed. Although she and Doug had been close friends for over fifteen years, it had been years since she had seen me in such high gear in business. I was driven to push forward. I had a keen sense that God was about to do a new work in our lives.

"Vicki, I have to tell you. Your faith amazes me. I never understood the scripture about faith moving mountains, but as you are speaking, I see how your faith is moving mountains. Do you realize how many mountains you are moving?"

Even as she spoke it, I had an immediate witness in my spirit. "You know, Greta, I have never thought about that scripture in those terms, but you are right. Faith does move mountains. There is no doubt about it."

As I hung up with her, I took a few minutes to contemplate all of the amazing ways God had moved since February 4th. An acquaintance I had known from our previous building ran into us at an Ad League luncheon. When I told him what we were up to, he asked me if I had ever attended a monthly networking breakfast of professionals in North Dallas. When I told him I had not even heard of it, he invited me to come as his guest to the next one, which just happened to be the next day.

At the networking breakfast, everyone got up and introduced him or herself and shared what they were doing. After the breakfast, I felt compelled to approach a woman who had described herself as a former Chief Operations Officer for a technical company. We met soon after that to discuss her coming on board with The Dot Com Agency in the same capacity.

During that same time period, I had called the President of TXU Communications to invite him over to our agency to see what we were doing. Over lunch, we discussed the contacts at TXU that we might introduce to our new agency concept. He was intrigued with our idea of bringing together the principals and their teams of small, specialized agencies to work on large projects for clients that needed a fast turnaround with the excellence of experienced professionals.

Before lunch was over, he had given me the name of the Internet Manager at TXU and suggested that I give her a call. I had called her before I left for an out of town trip, but she had not gotten back with me before I left. As I was leaving the office, I instructed our new Chief Operating Officer to please speak with her for me if she called.

As I was driving cross-country, I got a call from our new COO on my cell phone. It turned out that the Internet Manager at TXU was her good friend who had also attended the North Dallas networking group. After talking for awhile, she had confided that she did have a very exciting Internet marketing project coming up that required a very broad expertise in Internet marketing, public relations and media buying. Although they were planning on using a large general market agency for the project, she was not averse to allowing our agency to pitch the business. By the time I got home from my trip, I had a meeting set up with her assistant to discuss the details.

At the meeting, I was told that if we would like a shot at the business, we would have to do a great deal of speculative work up front. The project was sizeable and they wanted to be sure we could handle it. I agreed to write a marketing plan, media plan and launch plan for the new business free of charge. If they liked the plans and felt we had a grip on what their new Internet business was all about, they would consider us for the business.

Although I had my work cut out for me, I was riding high. I had chosen the small, specialty shops that I would bring into the business with me and tapped into their expertise as needed. I worked day and night, refining the three plans, until I felt confident that we had a winning strategy. Finally, I called TXU and told them I was ready to present our plans to their team. Instead of involving all of the other agencies in the presentation, I asked one of the potential team members to present with Paco and me. I knew in my spirit that we should not overwhelm them with people, just with ideas.

When the presentation was over, I knew we had won them over. Although there were still many questions to answer and another big meeting to present our plans again with all of the agency principals present, I was not fazed. It was a typical David and Goliath scene, as we fearlessly took on one of the largest agency networks in the world. When it was all said and done, our little team had won the business. As Greta said, "Our faith moved mountains." I was totally psyched and ready to pull up my sleeves and deliver the very best service this client group had ever seen. If God was for me, who could be against me?

We were up and running. We had less than three months to implement the strategies we had presented in the plan. As all of the small groups conferred in collaboration on the project, each one stepped up to the plate to deliver their very best product. Over the next three months, I worked tirelessly to oversee all of the details of each of the groups to be sure there were no snags.

Finally, the day of the launch had arrived. Everything went off without a hitch. The new president of the business services group sought me out at the event to thank me personally for a job well done. We had taken a nearly impossible task and completed it on time and on budget. I was proud of my team for their outstanding effort. As I looked back on all of the work that had to be completed in less than three months, I was fairly certain that the large agency never could have met the deadline. Just the processes and procedures alone would have killed them. I left the launch feeling very good.

Shortly before the launch, I had gotten a call from the Project Manager giving me a "heads up" on the fact that she and her assistant were being moved off of the project and that another project manager and agency contact person would be taking their place. Although I had met them briefly at the launch, I really had not gotten a sense about them. I was too busy with details to be worrying about our new working relationships with these people. I had faith that God would work it all out.

Now that the launch was over, it was time to fine-tune some of the final details of various events, promotions and public relations opportunities. I had not heard from anyone all week, which was fine with me since we had been so busy with the many minor details of the ongoing project. Finally, on late Friday afternoon, the new marketing coordinator called me at home. Since she was the main agency contact, I had given her all of my numbers so she could reach me anywhere, day or night, for any reason.

"Hi!" I said with genuine enthusiasm. "It is so nice to hear from you. Welcome to the team." My enthusiasm was met with stony silence. When she did speak, her tone of voice was cold and to the point.

"You will not be so excited to have me on your team a few months from now, Vicki. I won't go into it at this time. I just wanted to let you know that I will be calling you Monday morning. The new project manager has some grave concerns she has asked me to address."

As I hung up with her, a cold chill ran down my spine. "She really doesn't like me," I thought. I could not remember ever receiving such a venomous phone call. Just as I suspected, the fun was just beginning.

Monday morning, the call came. She was at her "other agency's office" and wondered if I had a contract with TXU so that I could fax it over to her other agency's fax number. In addition, she wanted clarification on everything our agency had done on the project and asked that we pull together binders with every detail of the project so that she and her project manager could review it. I definitely got the feeling we were guilty until proven innocent.

In the meantime, we were continuing to fulfill our part of the bargain, working feverishly to oversee the many events we had set up for our client. Just over a month after the launch, we were nearing the end of the events. My daughter, Jessica, had asked me to accompany her on a cross-country road trip to New York during her school break. We would be gone a week. With all of our ducks in a row on the account, I knew I could afford to be gone for a week. I had been working non-stop since the first of May. I welcomed the break.

We left on Saturday morning and arrived at my parents' house on Monday morning. Jessica and I spent the day riding around with my Dad, catching up with him on the welfare of family and friends. When I got back to their home, there were multiple messages from various team members, panicked over the events of the day. The client was suddenly very unhappy and an emergency phone conference had been held to discuss the details. The radio disc jockeys had disregarded our script and were "chatting" about the company in a way that was violating company rules. As much as I wanted to help, there was very little I could do from 1,500 miles away. I asked our account executive to call all of the stations and make certain the DJs understood the consequences of veering off of the written script.

After returning the phone calls, I sat down with my parents for some well-deserved rest and relaxation. There were still friends I wanted to ask about. "How is Mrs. Colborn doing these days?" I asked. "She has got to be in her mid-90s now, isn't she?"

"Oh, gosh yes!" Mom said. "She has been over in the nursing home area of Thompson Hospital for several years now."

"Bless her heart. She was such a wonderful woman. What is going to become of her beautiful Victorian home?"

"I don't know," Mom said. "But I know who would. Al Allen has been her maintenance man for years and still maintains the property. Let me give him a quick call and see what he can tell us."

When she hung up, she was full of information. Al had told my mom that the house had been vacant for several years as the attorneys were working on the papers for Mrs. Colborn's estate. That had all just been cleared up and there was a low-bid contract on the home that was to be accepted by Thursday if there were no other bidders. She had the name of the contact person, in the event I was interested in seeing the house.

I remembered the house well. I had been there often as a young pre-teen, taking voice lessons from the once great Betty Colborn. She had sung in the Philadelphia Opera and was a famous radio voice in her day. She was the first born-again Christian I had ever met that was open with her faith. When I became a Christian, she was one of the first people I stopped to tell when I went home to Upstate New York for a visit.

She clapped her hands and squealed with glee: "Oh gee, Vicki. You don't know how happy that makes me. I have been praying for you everyday for ten years!" I was struck to know that someone had been praying for me all of that time. No wonder I had to run forward that fateful day in 1979. Her prayers were being answered.

"I would like to see the house, Mom. Call the contact and see if you can get us in to see it tomorrow."

"Really, Vicki?" Mom said, incredulous at my interest. "Do you really think you may be interested in buying her house?"

"I don't know about that, but I sure would like to see it again. Do you mind calling the contact tonight to see if we can get in first thing in the morning?"

Within minutes, mom had the contact, Arden, on the phone and had arranged for a mid-morning showing on the house. Jessica was surprised that I would even consider the house. "What would you ever do with a house in Naples, Mom? We live in Dallas."

"I didn't say I was going to *buy* the house, Jessica. I just want to see it."

The next morning, the three of us met our contact at Betty's house. As Arden took us through the rooms, I did not feel anything in particular for the house. I was re-living memories of my voice lessons with Betty and her influence on my life, but I was not particularly impressed with the house. It was a fine Victorian home, resplendent with oak woodworking and flooring throughout, stained glass windows and impressive columns and window seats, but I could not see myself in it. We were modern, "great room" kind of people. I had never been a fan of Victorian houses. They were too confining for me.

"Thanks for showing us the house, Arden," I said, as I left. "Let me think about it and pray about it. I will call you one way or another in the next day or so."

On the way home, Jessica was pressing me for my reaction. "You are not really thinking of buying that house, are you, Mom? What would you do with it?"

"I told Arden I would pray about it and get back with her. I do not need or want that house. But if God wants us to have it for some purpose only known to Him, I am open to it. I have been a Christian long enough to know that you do not rule anything out with God."

Within 24-hours, I was positive that the Lord wanted me to buy the house. I had no idea why. In His wisdom, He didn't tell me why. But I knew beyond a shadow of a doubt that God was directing my path. He had brought us up to New York at this specific time for this specific purpose. Of that, I was certain.

Wednesday morning, I called Paco at work. "Honey, do you remember Betty Colborn's house, the large Victorian house on Main Street in Naples?"

"Of course I do, Vicki. I went there with you to visit her. What about it?"

"It is for sale through her estate. She is in a nursing home now."

"Yeah. What are you saying?"

"I am saying I went to see it yesterday with Mom and Jessica. After praying about it, I believe God has instructed me to buy it."

"Oh, come on, Vic. You cannot be serious. Why would God tell you to buy a house in Naples, NY? Our home and business are here in Dallas." He sounded irritated with me. I didn't blame him.

Although I could not imagine what God had in store for us, I knew we had to obey.

"Sweetheart, you have got to trust me. God has a plan. I don't know what it is, but He does. I am positive I have heard from the Lord on this. Please don't block what God wants to do in our lives. This is not the time to second-guess God."

Paco was quiet for a moment, as he took it all in. When he spoke, his voice had an air of resignation to it. "Whatever you think, Vic. If you believe God has told you to buy the house, then I guess that is fine. I just cannot imagine what we will ever do with it."

"If nothing else, we will sell it. I am sure it is priced below value and we could get our money out of it, then some. It is not a bad investment. Maybe God just wants to use us to bless Betty and her estate. She was one of the strongest Christian women I ever knew."

As I hung up with Paco, I looked over at my Dad. I had called Paco from the cell phone in his truck. "He gave me his blessing, Dad. I can buy the house." I extended my hand to clap his in a jubilant high-five. Dad looked at me with amazement, astonished that Paco would agree.

"Well if that doesn't beat all. You had better hurry up and turn that cell phone off before he changes his mind and calls back."

I knew God had moved in Paco's heart or he never would have agreed to allow me to buy the house. As excited as I was, my spirit was also troubled. "What does God know that I don't?" I mused. "What on earth are we ever going to do with an old Victorian house on Main Street in Naples?" Only God knew.

By Thursday afternoon, I had an accepted purchase offer on the house from the estate's attorney. It was a non-contingent offer for the amount the estate was requesting. I had a strong sense of accountability to Betty, as I knew if she were in her right mind, I would be submitting the offer to her personally. I did not want to do anything to dishonor this great woman of God. She had greatly impacted my life.

Within a week or two of my return to Dallas, we had the project we had been working on at TXU taken away from us. Although we had received kudos from every direction six weeks earlier, the project had taken a definite turn South when the new project manager and agency contact came on board. I fought the decision, but I knew in my spirit that the project had come to an end. It was a natural breaking point in the project, so we let it go.

As the year 2,000 wound down, our personal lives were definitely in transition. Elisa renewed her vows with her husband on New Year's Eve and Jessica was six months pregnant with her boyfriend's baby. David was attending a nearby college as a freshman during his junior year of high school. Our home demographics were changing rapidly.

Now there were just four of us at home, where once there had been seven. It almost felt as though we were the typical, all-American family. And yet, as Doug and Greta so often reminded us, there was absolutely nothing typical about us.

> *"But you are a chosen race, a royal priesthood, a dedicated nation, [God's] own purchased, special people, that you may set forth the wonderful deeds and display the virtues and perfections of Him Who called you out of darkness into His marvelous light."*
> *I Peter 2:9*

> *"Conduct yourselves properly (honorably, righteously) among the Gentiles, so that, although they may slander you as evildoers, [yet] they may by witnessing your good deeds [come to] glorify God in the day of inspection [when God shall look upon you wanderers as a pastor or shepherd looks over his flock]. Be submissive to every human institution for the sake of the Lord."*
> *I Peter 2:12,13*

> *"For one is regarded favorably (is approved, acceptable and thankworthy) if, as in the sight of God, he endures the pain of unjust suffering."*
> *I Peter 2:19*

CHAPTER 18

Resting In His Miracles

∝

In the spring of 2001, the Lord began to speak to me strongly about the transition He had in store for our business. Paco had been pulling the load for so long, he was starting to experience burn out. As I prayed about the situation, I felt the Lord leading us to simplify our lives and cut back to just the two of us in our business. By May, we had tied up all outstanding jobs and were free to take some time off. We decided to spend the time in the Colborn house in Naples, NY, enjoying the cool beginnings of summer.

Everyone but Elisa and Mickey were with us. Jessica and her three-month old son, Deacon, drove up separately with David. Paco and I followed with John and Daniel. It was a very magical time for our family, as we settled into the house in Naples to vacation for a few weeks. The large front porch was a great place to sit and rock and watch the world go by. It was as different from our lives in Dallas as night and day. The setting was picture perfect.

After just three weeks in Naples, we returned to Dallas. The Lord immediately began to speak to me about returning to Naples for one year. For the first time in a long time, the Lord was only revealing a small sliver of our next step. I knew I had heard His voice, but I was clueless as to why He would ask us to make such a sacrifice. Although we enjoyed the three-week stay, Dallas was where our home and business were located. Dallas was where we lived. How could we just up and leave for a year? There were too many financial sacrifices, not to mention risking our business reputation on such a move. Our entire financial lives were at stake.

"Lord," I prayed as I wrestled with Him night after night. "We cannot do this. I cannot do this. And I know, Paco will never agree to this. We just can't, Lord."

The Holy Spirit was unrelenting. "Vicki, you must. If you want to move forward in Me, you must obey, even at the risk of losing everything. Can you walk away from everything you own, everything you have become, for My sake?"

I wrestled for weeks with the Holy Spirit. I knew I had to place everything I had at the foot of the cross of Jesus. I had just made more money the previous year than I had ever made in my life. I was known in the high-level, corporate world in Dallas as a mover and a shaker. We had made a name for ourselves in the advertising industry in Dallas. I was the only female trustee at a church of thousands. We had worked ten years to get to this pinnacle in our lives. And now the Lord was asking me to just give it all up? It was mind boggling to me. And yet, I knew if the Lord was asking it of me, He had a plan. I had no option other than to obey the unction of the Holy Spirit and go.

"Lord, what if Paco refuses to come? I know he will never go for this."

Again, the Lord's instructions were clear. "Leave Paco in my hands. Trust me. If he refuses to go, you must go anyway." All of the theology I had ever learned about marriage ran contrary to what the Lord was saying. And yet I knew that I did not serve a cookie-cutter God. Jesus came to fulfill the law. I served a creative, loving God that was not confined to my theology.

"Okay, Lord. I will do it. I will obey You and go to New York."

When I explained to Paco the tug of war I had been having with the Lord, he was unsympathetic. "Vicki," he said. "I have put up with a lot over the years. And I know you hear from God. But I cannot do this. God has not spoken to me to do this. I just cannot pick up and go to New York and leave my business here."

"Honey, you never see your clients anyway. You sit in the corner of your office at a computer and send digital files. There is fast Internet in Naples. Your clients will understand if you work offsite. Just bring your computer and hook it up there and you are back in business."

"I cannot do that and I will not do that. If you feel like you have to go, go. But I cannot come. You have to understand my position."

Of course I did understand his position. I had been wrestling with all of the same issues myself. I could not imagine what God had planned. Why did I have to lay *my* marriage on the line? Our life in Dallas was everything I had ever wanted. Why did God have to upset the apple cart and ask me to do something so difficult?

As we drove away that fateful day in mid-July, my heart was breaking. I wept like an open wound as I made the 1,500-mile trek. My heart was aching and my spirit was crushed. I felt as though the pain ebbed and flowed from deep within the well of my spirit. Down in my soul, I knew that if God did not intervene, I would lose Paco forever. The reality of that thought unnerved me. Paco was the love of my life. He was my childhood sweetheart and my soul mate. Yet now that I had made this decision, my pleas for his love and affection were met with stony silence and cutting remarks. He was letting me know I had crossed the line.

I arrived in Upstate New York on Saturday morning and had found a church by Sunday. As I walked through the doors of the small church, the people that greeted me were open and loving. After the service, as I waited in line at the potluck lunch, I chatted with strangers that felt like brothers and sisters. I had never walked into a room of complete strangers and felt like I had made everyone's acquaintance beforehand. It was a totally new experience for me. I knew I had found my new spiritual home.

I threw myself into Bible study and fellowship with this new group of believers. From the depth of my spirit, I wanted to know and become known by my new church family. Their instant acceptance came at a time when I was feeling acute rejection from my husband and friends in Dallas. No one believed God would send me away from my husband for a year. Everyone I knew in Dallas was certain I had taken a major step outside of the perfect center of God's will.

As soon as I arrived in Naples, the Lord began to move in my life. Within days, I had received a notice from the IRS stating that I owed them $13,000 for a tax return they had not received from 1998. There was no tax due at the time; however, the penalty and interest that had accrued over the years for not submitting the return was $13,000. I stared at the bill in disbelief. I had been dealing with this issue for several months and had faxed back my reply. Having done all I knew to do, I was at a loss at what to do next.

The Wednesday after I arrived at the house in Naples, the church was meeting at a Bible Study in the pastor's home a few miles up the road. I was excited to attend, but did not feel I could share such a personal prayer request with people I really did not know yet. As the evening was wrapping up, the subject was turned to miracles of the Holy Spirit and how God comforts us with the Body of Christ.

One of the men in the group, Dennis, spoke up.

"I had my own business and had received a notice from the IRS that I owed them $13,000 for back taxes." He went on to say that his spirit was so heavy during this time as he carried with him the burden of knowing he had this insurmountable bill hanging over his head. His pastor at the time, not knowing what he was going through, had come up to him before the Sunday service and hugged him in a warm, loving embrace that just melted away every fear he had been harboring in his heart.

When he mentioned the exact figure that I was facing, my heart nearly stopped. I knew that the Lord was letting me know that he wanted this small band of faithful Christians to believe with me for a miracle. When Dennis had finished his story, I asked the group to pray for me to receive a miracle. I knew from the extensive phone conversation I had earlier in the day with my attorney on the subject, that the battle could be brutal. He had warned me that the IRS has an arsenal of lawyers. They can drag cases out for months and even years if they choose to fight you. He emphasized that fighting the IRS could be likened to fighting a well-equipped army with never ending supplies of ammunition. He had painted a dismal picture of a long, drawn-out battle. I knew if God did not intervene, I would most likely end up in a deadlock with the IRS. My heart had sunk like a rock just thinking about it.

Pastor Bert pulled out his anointing oil and asked me to sit on the cocktail table where the group could gather around me. As they all prayed for me, I felt a wonderful release in my spirit as my mind filled with peace. When the group stopped praying, Pastor Bert had a word of knowledge for me.

"Vicki," Pastor Bert said in his thick Peruvian accent. "The Lord would say to you: My child I am pleased with you. I have seen your tears. I have seen how your heart is breaking before Me. You have chosen to obey Me under difficult circumstances. For that I will reward you. Even now, I am erasing this debt. Just look to me and praise me, and watch as I move this mountain for you."

I knew even as the words were spoken, the Lord was moving mightily on my behalf. I had no doubt, as I left the Bible study that night, the case was closed. Less than two weeks later, I received a notice from the IRS stating that they had made a mistake and were very sorry for any inconvenience their error had caused me. Although I was elated, I was not surprised. I knew in my heart it was finished the night I was prayed for.

A few weeks later, in mid-August, I was preparing to leave the house for the Bible study at Pastor Bert's home. I was going through my usual "out the door" routine. I had just checked to be sure the door was locked and stopped to re-arrange the throw on the sofa. I had some audio tapes my friends Doug and Greta had given me before I left Dallas, sitting on the top of the radiator, about six or seven feet from where I was standing. I had placed them there almost as soon as I had arrived in mid-July, and often thought as I passed by them that I should listen to those tapes some time. This night, as I stood re-arranging the throw, the tapes suddenly flew off the radiator and landed directly at my feet. In amazement, I stooped down to pick them up.

"I guess the Lord really wants me to listen to these tapes," I thought, shaken by the strange event. I took them with me to the car and immediately put the first tape into the tape player. In all of my years of serving the Lord, I had never witnessed anything that even resembled that miracle. Instead of concentrating on the supernatural nature of the event, I focused on the fact that the Holy Spirit had definitely taken up residence within our home in Naples. I just hugged myself, as I meditated on how wonderful it was to be in the perfect center of God's will. I was very glad I had come. I had a strong premonition that everything was going to be okay.

The third week of September, Jessica and Deacon flew up to visit. She had just finished another quarter at the Art Institute of Dallas and had a week before classes were to begin again. David was excited to have Jessica visit and asked her if she would like to go to the youth Bible Study with him at Pastor Bert's house. She decided to take the baby with her. That night, as Jessica walked through the door, I immediately sensed a change in her countenance.

"How did the Bible Study go, Jess?"

"Great," she said. She was absolutely radiant. "Nathan, Pastor Bert's son, taught the class."

"Oh, yeah. He seems like such a nice guy."

"He is, Mom. Our eyes locked when we first saw each other and it was like something very special happened. It is hard to explain. I really liked him a lot."

I felt warm all over just thinking about the encounter. Jessica deserved better than what she had. She had been dating the same guy since she was fourteen and was in a dead-end relationship.

"So do you think you will see him again, Jess?"

"Oh, Mom, I hope so. I have never met anyone like him."

Just four weeks later, Paco and I had a wedding to attend in Dallas, so I flew down to attend the wedding with him. Jessica decided to postpone her education and come to Naples with the baby to live with us. Under great pressure from me, Paco grudgingly decided to drive up to Naples with me, to spend a few months with the family and work from the Naples house. As we watched our three sons adjust to living in a small town of 1,200 people, we enjoyed the beauty and the majesty of the fall foliage on the rolling hills. For the first time in a long time, I felt alive again. It was great to have Paco home.

By the end of November, Nathan proposed to Jessica. They planned to wed the first week of March. By the end of December, David had fallen in love with Nathan's sister, Rachel. Brother and sister were dating sister and brother.

"Okay, Lord, You are really moving fast here," I thought, as I meditated on how quickly He had moved in all of our lives since we had arrived in Naples. In just over five months, two of our children had found their soul mates. Although we had never met the Hallancia family before, we had so much in common. Bert was from Peru and Paco was from Mexico. Both Jeanine and I were from the same rural area of Upstate NY. They had five children, three boys and two girls, just like us. Both families were sold out to the Lord, born-again and spirit-filled Christians. David and Rachel had both been born at home with midwives. The similarities between the two families were uncanny.

"We never would have known about this wonderful family if I had not obeyed you Lord," I thought. God blessed our family in Naples with favor with our new church family and friends. Our neighbors, Arnie and Donna, were the finest, warmest, and most loving and giving couple we had ever had the privilege of knowing. Every way we turned, there was a blessing awaiting us. The favor and anointing God placed on our lives during that time was unmatched. It was twelve months our family will always remember with fondness.

As the time approached for us to move back to Dallas, I was in a quandary as what to do with the house. I knew God had told us to buy it, but I really did not know if He wanted us to sell it. We were willing to do whatever He instructed, knowing that He knew best. The last week of June, I became serious about asking the Lord for an answer. As I sought Him in earnest, I felt strongly that we were to call the couple we were bidding against when we first bought the house in the fall of 2001. I had attended 12 grades of school with Bruce, and he had told me to please let him know if we ever decided to sell it.

With a single phone call, the house was sold without a realtor. We had made money on the investment in addition to the many blessings we enjoyed for the year we spent in the house.

The house closed on August 6th, Pacquito's 20th birthday. As I started my long drive back to Dallas that day, I had plenty of time to contemplate all of the wonderful ways the Lord had blessed us over the past twenty years.

As I reflected on the goodness and amazing faithfulness of God, I couldn't help but wonder what else He had in store for me and for my family. It had been an eventful, adventuresome life so far. Neither Paco nor I could have ever even imagined how much the Lord had in store for us when He first drew us to Himself.

Even since the writing of this book, God has continued to perform amazing miracles in our lives. He is not finished with us yet. As our lives unfold before us, I have a very strong witness in my spirit that this story is definitely "to be continued..."

> *"And let the peace (soul harmony which comes) from Christ rule (act as umpire continually) in your hearts [deciding and settling with finality all questions that arise in your minds, in that peaceful state] to which as [members of Christ's] one body you were also called [to live]. And be thankful (appreciative), [giving praise to God always]. Let the word [spoken by Christ] (the Messiah) have its home [in your hearts and minds] and dwell in you in [all its] richness as you teach and admonish and train one another in all insight and intelligence and wisdom [in spiritual things and as you sing] psalms and hymns and spiritual songs, making melody to God with [His] grace in your hearts. And whatever you do [no matter what it is] in word or deed, do everything in the name of the Lord Jesus and in [dependence upon] His person, giving praise to God the Father through Him."*
>
> *Colossians 3:15-17*

PROLOGUE

Called to Write

∞

In the fall of 2002, I returned to my life in Dallas with the expectation that we would just pick up where we left off when I left in July 2001. The more phone calls I made and the more people I spoke with, it became very apparent that much had changed in the Dallas economy since we had left. In a way, I felt like I had just spent a year with the Peace Corps and returned to a war zone. Everywhere I looked, there was lack and suffering. Many of the advertising agencies in the Dallas area were experiencing the worst economic downturn since The Great Depression. Many others had gone out of business.

For Paco and me, it was a time of tremendous transition. We knew in our spirits, the economic recovery was going to take some time. With each passing day, I was growing increasingly concerned about our economic future. The predictions were dismal. It could take years for our business to turn around. There was not enough going on at the ad agency to keep me busy. Yet, I had no idea what the Lord wanted me to do next. Was I to change careers? Should I become an interior designer? A real estate agent? A life coach? A stockbroker? What did the Lord have for me, now that we were back in Dallas and our business was lagging? I was feeling totally lost and confused.

When a good friend invited me to a motivational seminar one day, I heard about a revolutionary way to identify, purchase and track stocks online. When the invitation to sign up for the two-day seminar came, I literally ran to the sign-up table. I knew I needed to do something quickly. This sounded like the perfect answer. I could become a day trader and a stockbroker. I was sure, as I sat in the seminar a few weeks later, I would be good at this new career.

That night, I walked into the house after an all day, intensive training session on stock trading. As I sat down with Paco on the couch and went over the thick manual that had been provided to me, I gave him an overview of my day, anxious to share how much I had learned. I assured him, as I explained the process, this could be a very lucrative career for me.

Although I was jumping up and down on the outside, secretly I was experiencing continual consternation. In my heart, I had no peace. Feeling pressured to do something *(anything!)* I had moved ahead with this new career. All along, however, I had a nagging feeling in my inner spirit that something was not quite right.

Just before climbing into bed that night, I turned the television to *The 700 Club.* The hosts were praying for their viewers. At that very moment, Terry Meeuwsen had this word of knowledge:

"There are some of you who have just a lot of consternation in your hearts and minds about the purchase of homes right now, about the future of your academic pursuits. For some of you, it may even have to do with marriage, with relationship to someone; and there is such confusion in your heart and mind.

'Be still and know that I am God,' is the word from the Lord. Get into your prayer closet. Get on your knees. Get into the word of God and do nothing, nothing until God speaks to you. Do not let others rush you into things or give you easy answers or solutions. Your word will come from the Lord, and it will come directly to you. Wait on God for that."

My heart nearly stopped. I knew the word was for me. "Paco," I exclaimed. "That word is for me. The Lord is speaking to *me.*"

The next day, as I drove to the second day of the seminar, I felt lighter. I knew in my heart, if I was honest with myself and with the Lord, I had not been called to be a stockbroker and a day trader. He had called me to something else. But what? I still did not know. However, this one thing I did know. Until He spoke to me personally, I had to discontinue my career change. He would provide for our needs during our transition, just as He always had. I just had to be patient and wait for His instructions to me.

Less than a month had passed when the Lord called me to write down all that He had done in my life. He spoke to me clearly, saying: "I gave you the grace to live it; now I will give you the grace to write it." True to His word, He gave me amazing grace.

May God bless you and keep you as you go in peace, believing God at His Word. He is faithful and true. What He has done for me, He can do for you. Just remember, He is waiting for *you.*

The Green Reader Story

❧

U nbeknownst to me, during the same time that the Lord was working on my heart to write this book, He was giving Paco a vision of a training tool for golfers. The week before I was to go to a small cottage on Canandaigua Lake in Upstate New York to finish writing the book, Paco got busy applying for a patent over the Internet. Eight weeks later, as I was driving into Dallas, Paco called me on my cell phone to let me know he had just received official notice that the application had been filed and a patent was pending. Later I was to learn that Paco had actually received the idea nearly a year earlier, during the same time I was struggling with the Lord's call to write down all of the miracles He had performed in our lives. It seemed the two projects from the Lord were intertwined.

Paco and I were still struggling financially and had not received paychecks since December 2001. Twenty-four months later, our savings account was nearly exhausted. With mounting concerns about our future income and outgo, it took a giant leap of faith to fund Paco's new project with the small remainder of our personal savings.

In faith, we hired a small manufacturer in mid-December 2003 to draw up the device on the computer and create a prototype. Less than a month later, we had a prototype we could actually see and touch. We spent the next thirty days or so sharing it with various people, getting a feel for whether or not the product had merit and appeal. The more we showed it around, the more evident it became that the Lord had truly anointed the product. Nearly every person we showed it to wanted one as soon as we had some to sell.

Finally, the second week of February, I felt a call from the Lord to get involved in the project. I had just finished the process of sending my manuscript to the publishers, when the Lord began to reveal to me how special Paco's project really was.

The day was February 10th, and I had just come from a woman's ministry luncheon. For some reason, the morning had been very difficult for me emotionally and all through lunch I struggled with a deep sense of heaviness. After lunch, rather than go to the office, I felt I needed to go back home. I just wanted to lie down and shake off the heaviness I had been feeling all day. Before I went to my bedroom to lie down, I decided to check my e-mail. The same friend that had invited me to the motivational seminar was encouraging me to check out a website on web marketing that he thought we would enjoy. He didn't even know I had purchased a web address for our golf-training tool. He was thinking of our ad agency website when he referred me to the site.

As I perused the website, voraciously consuming a myriad of creative ideas for marketing a product on the Internet, I felt a tremendous lifting in my spirit. In an instant, I knew intuitively that I had found our answer. We could sell The Green Reader directly to golf enthusiasts over the web and bypass the traditional methods of launching a new product. Best of all, the marketing strategy required very little cash.

The next few days I was a new woman. I was praying for direction on The Green Reader almost continually. I needed more pieces to the puzzle if we were to continue in faith. I begged God to show me more of His plan for our product. Just a day or so later, I encouraged Paco to make the call to Hank Haney's office. He had been procrastinating, although we were both sure this famous golf instructor was the perfect choice for a celebrity endorsement on the product. The next day, Paco had an e-mail back from Hank. We had a meeting set for one week later.

Once again, our faith was in motion, moving mountains.

In the wee hours of the morning on February 14th, the Lord woke me up from a sound sleep. I knew He was calling me to get up and pray. As I went to the couch to pray, the Holy Spirit began to pour creative ideas into my spirit. For the next few hours, I sat on the couch writing and praying. I felt like a secretary, taking dictation from her boss. The faster I wrote, the faster He seemed to speak. Finally I went back to bed, exhausted from the exercise. The Lord repeated this process in my life night after night for nearly three weeks. Some nights I wrote furiously. Other nights I just prayed for a few hours. Other nights I would read the Word. A few nights, He just ministered to my spirit and I would sit and weep. It was an intense time with the Lord unlike anything I had ever known.

Those weeks were a whirlwind. As the Lord continued to minister to me in the early morning hours, I felt totally infused with His faith during the day. In perfect faith that the money would come, I set about to line up the third-party vendors I knew we would need to make our product a success. The Lord showed me that this was to be a family business and that each of our five children was to be involved in the partnership. Although our three oldest were scattered all over the U.S., each one readily agreed to come back to Dallas to work in the business as soon as they could get home in the spring.

When Paco and I met with Hank to test our product, he was obviously impressed. Several times he and his manager asked Paco how he came up with such a great idea. Although Hank verbally agreed to endorse it, it would be ten days later before I would get the e-mail confirming his commitment. The entire time I was fighting a heavenly battle. I clung to the scripture that says: "the weapons of our warfare are not carnal, but mighty through God to the pulling down of strongholds, casting down imaginations and every high thing that exalts itself against the knowledge of God, bringing into captivity every thought to the obedience of our Lord Jesus Christ".

One of the directives I had from the Lord during that time was to give a 30-day notice at the end of February to our tenants whose 2 BR apartment adjoined our office space. He assured me we would need that space for The Green Reader offices. When I shared the Lord's directive with Paco, he was uncomfortable letting a good-paying tenant go when we needed the income to offset our expenses. I assured him I had heard from God, and in faith, I prepared the 30-day termination papers. The next Friday morning, I came to the office prepared to serve the notice. To my surprise and delight, our tenant of five years had served us a notice that he would be vacating the premises within the next few weeks. That was just one of the miracles the Lord did for us during that time.

Just a few days later, on my 48th birthday, I had several other miracles. My day started with a message from Hank confirming he would endorse The Green Reader. Later that day, I received a phone call from the coordinator of the Key Executive monthly meeting at Hillcrest. "Vicki", he said. "I got your phone message yesterday about your desire to speak at the Key Executive meeting this May. You probably didn't know when you made that request that we have been booked a year in advance for some time now. What I wanted to tell you is how timely that phone call was. At the exact same time you were leaving a message on my office phone requesting to speak at the May meeting, I received a call from our May speaker on my cell phone saying something had suddenly come up and he would be unable to speak in May. So we would love to have you speak at the May meeting." As I hung up, I felt warm all over. It had been a birthday unlike any other. "Thank you, Jesus", I thought, "for making a way where there seemed to be no way." Little did I know, that was just the beginning of what the Lord had planned for Paco and me and our family.

The Green Reader business literally changed our lives. Once again the Lord had created something out of nothing and rewarded our faithfulness to move forward on a prompting from Him in total faith. Using the money from an IRA we rolled over, we had believed God for a miracle. It wasn't the first time we had clung to the Lord's revealed will in our lives and the power of His Word. Or that He had rewarded our obedience.

For the first time in many years, I was reminded of a prophecy that was spoken over Paco and me less than two months after our infant son died in 1982. Harry and Jo, traveling prophets, had been visiting the Dallas area. We were sitting in a living room where they were ministering. Harry pointed to me and said, "You have a sister. She looks just like you." (He couldn't have known, since he never met her, that my sister Marcia and I were often mistaken for each other.) Later, he continued, "...you and your husband will climb the mountain and climb the mountain and climb the mountain and climb the mountain and climb the mountain. Then you will come to the top of the mountain. And you will have come to the place where every valley shall be lifted and filled up and every mountain and hill shall be made low; and the crooked and uneven shall be made straight and level and the rough places a plain. And the glory and majesty of the Lord will be revealed in your lives. Thus saith the Lord, as you trust upon My son and your savior, Jesus Christ."

Finally, we had made it to the mountaintop. Just as He promised, the Lord had made the crooked paths straight and the rough places smooth. To God be the glory for the great things He has done. Amen.

"For if anyone listens to the Word without obeying it and being a doer of it, he is like a man who looks carefully at his [own] natural face in a mirror. For he thoughtfully observes himself, and then goes off and promptly forgets what he was like. But he who looks carefully into the faultless law, the [law] of liberty, and is faithful to it and perseveres in looking into it, being not a heedless listener who forgets but an active doer [who obeys], he shall be blessed in his doing (his life of obedience)."

James 1:23-25

"Now faith is the assurance (the confirmation, the title deed) of the things [we] hope for, being the proof of things [we] do not see and the conviction of their reality [faith perceiving as real fact what is not revealed to the senses]."

Hebrews 11:1

Printed in the United States
18445LVS00003B/67-255

9 781594 673047